THE HEART OF
BRANSON

THE HEART OF
BRANSON

THE ENTERTAINING FAMILIES OF AMERICA'S
LIVE MUSIC SHOW CAPITAL

ARLINE CHANDLER

Foreword by Raeanne Presley, Mayor of Branson

THE
History
PRESS

Published by The History Press
Charleston, SC   29403
www.historypress.net

Copyright © 2010 by Arline Chandler
All rights reserved

First published 2010

Manufactured in the United States

Back cover, top center and top right: Photos by Lee Smith.

ISBN 978.1.60949.004.1

Chandler, Arline.
The heart of Branson : the entertaining families of America's live music show capital /
Arline Chandler.
p. cm.
Includes index.
ISBN 978-1-60949-004-1
1. Musicians--Missouri--Branson--Biography. I. Title.
ML394.C47 2010
781.64209778'797--dc22
2010036876

*To my granddaughter, Jasmine Linn, who grew up loving Silver Dollar City,
and to my aunt, the late Altha Chastain, who grew old loving the Presleys.*

CONTENTS

Foreword

If you are a loyal Branson fan, or just curious about what makes this Ozarks town unique, *The Heart of Branson: The Entertaining Families of America's Live Music Show Capital* will more than satisfy. I have admired Arline Chandler's writing talent for many years. She has documented the growth of Branson's tourism industry in ways that are both entertaining and informative. We are blessed that she shares her gift. Years ago, I remember an article that she wrote for our family business, Presleys' Country Jubilee. I could see the sparkle of the sequined costumes, smell the buttered popcorn and hear the strum of the guitar! Now, it is your turn to lose yourself in the history and culture of Branson and these holy Ozarks hills.

When my parents retired in 1968, our family moved to Branson. We made our home on Roark Creek, just a stroll away from beautiful Lake Taneycomo. I clearly remember barefoot summers and nickel ice cream cones at the Alexander Drug Store in the heart of historic downtown Branson. The rest of my story includes my marriage into the talented Presley family and my election as the first female mayor of Branson in 2007. While I would not pretend to know all that is Branson, I see that Arline has chronicled the timeline of our town with a personal and humorous touch. Branson has many people to thank for its success. Through this book you will come to know the families and individuals who built Branson and the friends who bring new talents and ideas to our tourism world. Hopefully, you will understand how we strive to keep family values alive for both our residents and visitors.

I truly love our authentic Branson. In this book I see reflected the struggles and successes of our community. As you step into our lives in the pages of this book, I hope you will find reasons to celebrate your own hometown traditions. As mayor, my role is to help guide the future of Branson. My goal is that we will find a way to continue to respect our past and keep true to our mission of championing family, faith, friends and flag—forever.

Thank you, Arline, for honoring us with this book and truly capturing the heart of Branson.

Raeanne Presley
Mayor of Branson

ACKNOWLEDGEMENTS

This book would not have been possible without the help of my life partner, Lee Smith, who formatted the photographs and spent hours in the final editing. My sincere thanks to Lisa Rau and Martha Bohner, publicists for Silver Dollar City, who answered my questions and gathered photos and research materials.

Over the past thirty years, I have had the privilege to interview many of the individuals named in this book. My special thanks to Jack Herschend, Rex Burdette and Brad Thomas for recent conversations about Silver Dollar City. Thank you to Gary and Pat Snaden, owners of Shepherd of the Hills Homestead—with Sharena Naugher, public relations; Keith Thurman, drama director; and Jeannie Skrzeczkoski, tour guide—for recounting history.

Thank you to Lynn Berry, director of public relations; Kim Heminger, media relations manager; and Dan Lennon, vice-president, marketing and public relations, of the Branson/Lakes Area Chamber of Commerce and Convention and Visitors Bureau. They answered questions and provided insights into the Branson music scene. Thank you, Dan, for the interview.

To Hollye Gurley, publicist for the Baldknobbers; Angie Harris, publicist for the Hughes Brothers; Chris Dodson, publicist for the Haygoods; and Laura M. Sanford, Image Works, Inc., thank you for your help in obtaining photos and information. My appreciation goes out to Raeanne Presley for writing the foreword and to members of the Presley family who answered requests for information. Thank you, Sheila and Judith Dutton, for your time and for answering my questions and sending photos.

Acknowledgements

Thank you to writer Suzanne Wilson for sharing information about S. Fred Prince and to Prince's granddaughter, Charlotte Al-hujazi, who gave permission for quotes from her grandfather's unpublished manuscript, "The Ozarkian Uplift and Marvel Caverns."

To the numerous entertainers I have had the privilege to enjoy onstage over the last three decades, I give my appreciation—and my applause. Thank you for making Branson a breath of fresh air in the entertainment world.

Introduction

We live in the present, we dream of the future, but we learn eternal truths from the past.
—Lucy Maud Montgomery

In the early 1900s, rock ledges and rutted trails served as roads, isolating the Missouri Ozarks from the nation's progress following World War II. The Branson entertainment story started on the front porches of log cabins— beating its rhythm to the strum of a washtub bass, the slap of kitchen spoons in a lap and a bow drawing over fiddle strings in a lilting tune. Families "made do" with handmade tools, homegrown food, hand-sewn clothing and homespun entertainment. In the first half of the twentieth century in the forty-seven thousand square miles of highlands called the Ozarks in southern Missouri, northern Arkansas and northeast Oklahoma, hill families lived in a time warp. Their culture, language and traditions fascinated outsiders.

Silver Dollar City's general manager, Brad Thomas, reflected: "Before Table Rock Lake and the boom of tourism, life was hard in the Ozarks. Thin soil covered rocky hillsides. Homesteaders could grow watermelons, berries and tomatoes—a sparse living on three crops with a short growing season."

Tourism began as early as 1894 when a few adventurous people toured Marble Cave, later named Marvel Cave. The White River Railroad Line, running from Carthage, Missouri, to Newport, Arkansas, in the early 1900s, opened up transportation for curious travelers. After *Shepherd of the Hills* was published in 1907, train passengers hired taxi drivers from Branson to tour them through the isolated hill country over narrow roadways with names such as "The Trail Nobody Knows How Old." Power Site Dam, built across the White River in 1913, backed up Lake Taneycomo and drew fishermen. In 1921, Fairy Cave (now Talking Rocks Cavern) opened for tours. Still, a lack of roads meant seclusion for the region.

From 1933 to 1958, Jim Owen, a local fisherman, operated a float service, especially on the White River prior to the building of Bull Shoals, Beaver and Table Rock Dams. He and his native Ozarks guides launched johnboats, carrying as many as ten thousand guests over the years, to view unspoiled scenery and dip fishhooks into pristine waters. His adventures drew visitors to the Ozarks, creating jobs for boat builders, guides and vendors, who supplied food for his campfire meals. The tall tales spun on the White River's gravel bars came with the excursion price.

Owen built Branson's first movie theater and lured film actors and producers to vacation in the Ozarks. As Branson's mayor, he tirelessly promoted the Ozarks, cultivating contacts with writers and photographers, resulting in mentions and cover stories in national sports and general interest magazines. By 1959, the Mabe brothers started Branson's first music show to cash in on the stream of fishermen and their families lured to Branson.

Pete Herschend, co-owner of Silver Dollar City, stated that three things simultaneously came together in 1960 to propel tourism in Branson, Missouri, to its current status as a family entertainment destination. "Table Rock Lake filled. Press in the regional media about the fishing, camping and water recreation brought an influx of people," he said. "The Shepherd of the Hills Homestead started its outdoor drama based on Harold Bell Wright's book. And Silver Dollar City opened. Those three things were not planned to coincide. They simply happened."

However, Silver Dollar City's general manager, Brad Thomas, believes that there is another part of that story worth telling: the fact that in Branson, the "home runs" among theaters, businesses and theme parks happened when entrepreneurs worked shoulder to shoulder. He says:

> *Entertainment businesses do compete, but we all win when we bring more visitors to this market. I love the story of the mid-1970s, when the oil embargo created actual gas shortages. Tourists did not know if they could buy gas at the local pumps. Talk about scary times. Branson is dependent on people arriving in their cars, RVs and tour buses.*
>
> *Pete Herschend and other local individuals got together and procured gas. They made the promise to visitors: "If you drive to Branson, we guarantee you can purchase gas to get back home." That wasn't a boom summer for Branson, but it certainly kept it from being a ghostly town.*

Thomas notes that particular time when businesses cooperated set a precedent for working together. After that summer, business owners formed the Ozark Marketing Council, which later turned into the Branson/Lakes Area Chamber of Commerce and Convention and Visitors Bureau.

Prior to the 1990s, scarcely anyone beyond Tulsa, Oklahoma; Kansas City; or St. Louis, Missouri, knew about Branson's wholesome, family-oriented entertainment at Silver Dollar City, Shepherd of the Hills Homestead and a handful of theaters along Highway 76. In 1991, Morley Safer broke the story on CBS's *Sixty Minutes*, asking questions: "Why Branson, Missouri? Why is this small town in the Ozarks becoming the entertainment capital of America?"

Why, indeed. In his report, Safer missed Branson's heartbeat—families entertaining families. He missed a tradition that reached back to Marble Cave and entrepreneurs such as William Lynch, Hugo Herschend, Jim Owen, the Mabe brothers and the Presley family. He missed the "one for all" attitude of businesses. Most of all, he missed the genuine caring for people, the contagious lighthearted fun, the hard work ethic and the hill folk integrity that had passed from generation to generation and built the platform on which Branson stands today.

CHAPTER 1

IN THE BEGINNING

Holes in the Mountains

Caves are so numerous in the Ozarks that they form the rocky skeleton of the hills.
—Phyllis Rossitor, A Living History of the Ozarks,
used by permission of the publisher, Pelican Publishing Company, Inc.

A young hunter spears a bear and falls through a dark hole in the Ozark Mountains…Osage kinsmen call the place "Devil's Den"…Ponce de León seeks the Fountain of Youth in the mysterious cavern…tales of gold coins…legends of Spanish prisoners escaping a cave's chamber over a ladder of human bodies…miners explore the mountain's dark recesses for lead… reports of marble ceilings…hill folk called the cavern "Marble Cave"…a Confederate guerilla is pitched over the edge by Ozarks vigilantes…whispers of a "Dead Animal Room."

Folklore and, later, newspapers and magazines romanticized these legends about the sinkhole atop Roark Mountain near Branson, Missouri. No one knows if a science magazine's report of prehistoric bones prompted Canadian William Lynch to pay the tidy sum of $10,000, sight unseen, for this seemingly worthless hole in the ground. Nonetheless, he left a promising career as a dairyman, mining expert and Canadian government official to pursue a dream. Packing meager household furnishings on mules, and accompanied by two unmarried daughters, Miriam and Genevieve, he journeyed in 1893 to claim ownership of Marble Cave.

According to Dave Houston in a *Missouri Business* article (1977), Lynch expected fame and fortune from the bones on the cave's floor. After New York's Museum of Natural History thanked him in words for his contribution,

Above left: William T. Lynch purchased Marble Cave in 1893. *Courtesy of Silver Dollar City Archives.*

Above right: Marble Cave entrance, with wooden ladder from the top of the sinkhole to the debris pile. *Courtesy of Silver Dollar City Archives.*

he turned to simple survival in an isolated part of the Ozark Mountains. The Lynch family committed fifty years to developing a natural wonder into a show cave, initiating the Ozarks tradition of families entertaining families.

In a state famous for caves, Missouri's deepest cavern is appropriately the starting point for Branson's tourism. A faded ribbon from the grand opening of Marble Cave in Onyx Park on October 18, 1894, rests in the archives at Silver Dollar City. The only improvement for that grand day was a wooden ladder extending down the ninety-four-foot sinkhole and resting on the mountain of debris swept naturally through the sinkhole's mouth and hardened by eons of limestone falling from the ceiling. Evidence of a platform in the west passage led to speculation that the Lynch sisters had a piano lowered through the cave entrance. Miriam Lynch, a trained opera singer, likely entertained the guests with arias and piano music. No one knows whether the explorers, wet and muddy after sliding down slopes and crawling through clay-packed tunnels, appreciated the refined music.

Traces of the Past

After the Osages slashed a sideways "V" at the opening to warn of evil, no recorded person entered the cave until 1869, when Henry T. Blow, a lead mining magnate from St Louis, and a few explorers lowered themselves into the hole in the mountain. In 1883, Truman S. Powell, T. Hodges Jones and other men from Lamar, Missouri, explored the property and formed the Marble Cave Mining and Manufacturing Company, expecting to mine treasured marble. However, the company's geologist confirmed that the ceilings and walls were mere limestone. Massive piles of bat guano (droppings), twenty-five feet tall, proved the only valuable resource. To recoup their investment, the miners lowered ore carts and donkeys into what is today called the Cathedral Room. They mined out the guano, which brought $700 per ton for the manufacture of gunpowder and fertilizer. A pulley system lifted heavy buckets loaded with "black gold" out of the cave. Nonetheless, the donkeys fared poorly, and most died of pneumonia.

After four and a half years, Marble Cave Mining terminated all operations, leaving the buildings above the cave deserted. The mining venture had created a platted town called Marble City—later named Marmaros, the Greek word for marble. The bustling village boasted a hotel, a general store, a pottery shop, a white oak furniture factory, a school and, rumor has it, a saloon. Marmaros was a stagecoach stop between Springfield, Missouri, and Berryville, Arkansas.

When the Lynches arrived on the scene, they discovered that the old frame buildings had burned to the ground, leaving only moss-covered stone foundations and practically no trace of the citizens whose steps fell silent. Ozarks lore tells that a vigilante group, the Bald Knobbers, torched the buildings—perhaps in protest of "foreigners" buying up property in their mountains.

A Self-taught Artist-Scientist Surveys the Cave

About the same time, S. Fred Prince from Chicago wandered into the Ozarks. Marble Cave's owner asked the newcomer to survey his cave. Prince devised homemade instruments for the job. He wrote, "In a few weeks, I knew more about the inside of the country than I ever did of its surface, and it absorbed most of my life for ten years."

In his illustrated but unpublished manuscript, "The Ozarkian Uplift and Marvel Caverns" (1893–1942), he described the cave room by room, writing that he learned to read the wonderful story inscribed in their rocks and the spaces between—the story of the beginnings of a new world.

Prince's initial survey took two years. His handwritten manuscript and meticulous pencil sketches possibly were recorded over forty-nine years. In his words:

> *We put up a tent in the Cathedral Room, and even built a stone fireplace, and lived down there for weeks or months at a time. Mr. Lynch kept me supplied with life's necessities.*
>
> *In the deeper and more remote places, I would often, when tired, simply stretch out where I was and rest. And then go on with the work. There was no change, just even darkness, even, unchanging temperature and moisture, and a blessed stillness!*

Prince describes William T. Lynch as a kind man devoted to helping all about him. "He was the real pioneer of this country, recognizing its beauty and its need of development," Prince wrote in his book. "He was the first to work for the betterment of its roads, and spent a large portion of his time and money on them and on making the dream of a railroad come true."

MARBLE CAVE BECOMES A MARVEL FOR TOURISTS

In the following years, Marble Cave became Marvel Cave, perhaps because the Lynch sisters thought that "Marvel" more poetically described the wonderland beneath the mountain. S. Fred Prince penned, "The name 'Marble Cave' was untrue. Marvel was all truth and dignity." Prince also noted that William Lynch opposed the name change. However, by 1918, the *Stone County News-Oracle* consistently referred to the attraction as Marvel Cave. Lynch himself called his property Marvel Cave when he advertised it for sale that year, giving his address as Reeds Spring.

At that time, roads in the southwestern Ozarks were rutted trails over limestone shelves that followed the curvy spine of mountain ridges. Early visitors from as far away as Kansas City and Chicago rode a train to Springfield, about fifty miles north of Branson, and traveled by horseback or wagon to the cave. In 1906, the White River Line of the St. Louis and Iron Mountain Railroad steamed down Roark Valley into Branson. Still, transportation from Branson to Marvel Cave covered rugged terrain. Lynch started clearing ten miles of roadway into Branson, making the trail level enough for wagons and automobiles. Repairs, especially around Dewey Bald, were continuous. Often, Lynch himself traveled to town and hauled guests back to the cave. For five dollars, he offered transportation to and from the cave, a tour and overnight room and board.

In 1920, the railroad opened a line running west from Branson. Lynch negotiated a flag stop called Roark Station at which travelers could detrain and then ride a horse or hike to the cave. Following their adventure, they returned to their coach. Also by 1920, a witty, enterprising woman, Pearl Spurlock, operated a taxi service up over a trail road that climbed the rocky shoulder of Dewey Bald into what she called "Shepherd of the Hills

Early visitors to Marble Cave. *Courtesy of Silver Dollar City Archives.*

Country." In her book *Over the Old Ozark Trails*, she claimed that she ferried passengers from all over the United States and numerous foreign countries through the bumpy countryside approaching Marvel Cave.

In the early tours, folks backed down the rickety ladder and viewed the natural wonders by candlelight. Silver Dollar City co-owner Jack Herschend said that "the Lynches considered kerosene lanterns too risky, so they provided candles to visitors up until 1932. Tours required six hours. At the surface, they outfitted guests in coveralls with leather seats for sliding down muddy passages."

The adventuresome souls who descended into the inky darkness of the Cathedral Room, which is recognized as one of the largest cave entrance rooms in North America, believed the tour to be worthy of their ticket money, their time and significant strenuous effort. The room measures more than 200 feet in height and 225 feet in width and is 400 feet long. Guides led them past a formation known as the Liberty Bell and down the winding Serpentine Passage to the Egyptian Room. The linear layers of rock on the

Genevieve Lynch, second from left, with 1913 exploration party into Marble Cave, later named Marvel Cave. *Courtesy of Silver Dollar City Archives.*

chamber's walls reminded the Lynch sisters of Egyptian architecture. They often called the flat ceiling "Cleopatra's sandal," indicative of today's name, the Shoe Room.

Lacking modern-day handrails and concrete steps, tours crept down the Corkscrew, past the Gulf of Doom and into the Waterfall Room. Flickering candles cast strange shadows on the stone walls. Fluttering bats and water rushing over ledges deep in the cave unleashed imaginations of voices calling out names and winged creatures whooshing overhead.

Until 1958, cave tours ended at the Waterfall Room. Visitors retraced their steps over half a mile to the cavern's entrance. In the early tours, comparable to today's spelunking, visitors grasped pickaxes to climb their way over the mountain of debris to return to daylight.

HILL FOLK AT THE CAVE

Early on, Mr. Lynch hired fifteen-year-old Fannabelle Ford (who later became Fannabelle Nickel) to assist his daughters, Miriam and Genevieve, as cave guides. Fannabelle helped to fit visitors with overalls for the tours. Since the cave served as refrigeration for guests' meals at the lodge the Lynches had built, she carried both food and spring water up from the cave's depths.

Rex Johnson, a young barefoot (and often shirtless) boy from the Marble Cave School, signed on with the family operation. Johnson spent days trekking over Ozarks hills with S. Fred Prince while the self-educated naturalist sketched wildflowers and ferns.

Mr. Lynch also hired nine-year-old Lester Vining to help him clear the rutted roadway that later became Missouri Highway 76. Oral accounts relate that Vining earned an apple and one quarter per day. However, Vining's daughter, Betty Rantz, thinks that her father likely worked for food only, planting a rosebush or hacking brush for the road.

"My dad, the son of the character Fiddlin' Jake in *The Shepherd of the Hills* story, lived a hardscrabble childhood," she says. "Growing up myself around the Lynch sisters, I believe their hearts went out to this raggedy, disheveled little boy. One of my overriding impressions of the Misses Lynch is that they cared about children."

Rantz's second most prominent memory of the Lynch sisters wraps around their love and knowledge of plants. She says:

Fannabelle Nickel with Levi Morrill, postmaster at Notch, Missouri. Morrill inspired the character of Uncle Ike in *Shepherd of the Hills. Courtesy of Silver Dollar City Archives.*

> *They knew the Latin names. Yet, they never looked down their noses at any of us hill folk. Miss Genevieve taught many about nature, caves and conversational French.*
>
> *Their house revealed an English influence with nooks and crannies and rock walls, a romantic, cultural place in my childhood mind. They lived and conducted business in the Ozarks during a time when women had little say in matters. Yet, after their father died in 1927—two women living alone—I never recall anyone threatening or taking advantage of them.*

After ownership of the cave passed to the Misses Lynch, Genevieve—a trained nurse and a poet with published works—left her career as a hospital administrator in Carthage, Missouri, to help Miriam carry on their father's dream. They added wooden steps and railings at the cave's entrance. Visitors no longer backed down a ladder.

The Lynch ladies opened guest cottages and a tearoom that served full meals. Often, they entertained friends such as Rose O'Neill, creator of the

Miriam Lynch (with parasol) greets guests at Marvel Cave Lodge. *Courtesy of Silver Dollar City Archives.*

Kewpie, and her mother Meemie, carrying on lively conversations well after the dark of night. For half a century, the Lynch family hosted other families in the Ozarks.

Most historic photos show Genevieve in blue jeans with Wellington boots up to her knees. Jack Herschend remembers Miriam as "refined—a gentle lady who read extensively." He says that the well-educated sisters shared a love of learning.

"These dear friends were different from anybody I'd ever met," he adds. "Their company sustained my mother during those early years as manager of the cave. I remember them for friendship, not simply [as] business associates."

Lester Vining, Fannabelle Nickel and Rex Johnson continued working for the Lynches and later for the Herschends until the 1960s and 1970s. Their resourcefulness in early days lives in an oft-told tale about a cow grazing too close to the sinkhole and falling with a loud crash to her death. Thinking that the cave had collapsed, Lester, Fannabelle and Rex left half-eaten lunches and raced to the cave. They pondered how to haul that dead cow up the ladder to the top of the sinkhole. Offering free beef to nearby farmers could be the answer, they determined. Fannabelle ran to spread the word, while

Rex and Lester butchered the cow. Neighbors, thrilled to have fresh meat, carried out the misfortunate animal one piece at a time.

Jack Herschend remembers the Lynches' gunnysack system for bookkeeping hanging behind the door. Cave tour tickets cost $1.25, a hefty sum in Depression days. "At that time, there was a 20 percent federal amusement tax, plus a three-cent sales tax," he says. "Into gunnysack number one, they put $1.02 from every ticket sold. Gunnysack number two held twenty cents, and gunnysack number three held the remaining three cents. All operational bills were paid from gunnysack number one. The moneys in sacks two and three went to the appropriate government agencies. Times were simple back then."

AN UNDERGROUND FAIRYLAND

While tourists took in the wonders of Marvel Cave, two young boys hunting with their dogs ran a rabbit under a ledge back in the mountains around Reeds Spring. Walker Powell, grandson of Truman S. Powell—one of the stockholders of Marble Mining Company—says that the rabbit likely was the boys' supper, so they pulled back the rock in pursuit and discovered a barrel-sized entrance to a cave. They threw rocks down the dark hole and listened to a silent echo. Word of the mysterious hole in the mountainside spread among Ozarks families, yet no one explored.

Three years later on a warm June Saturday, Truman S. Powell sat on a seat fashioned from a strong oak branch tied on the end of a one-hundred-foot rope. Four of his stoutest neighbors operated a pulley, secured to the center of a windlass and built on two forked logs. Slowly, the men lowered Powell through a slit under the overhanging ledge inadvertently discovered by the teenagers.

After his first descent, Powell made the statement that "the rocks visually speak to me." Back in 1896, this newspaper man had earned the distinction of being the Ozarks' resident cave expert. No doubt he possessed a kinship with the worlds he explored beneath rugged hillsides. He wrote many articles and stories about Marvel Cave. His descriptions were often picked up in far-flung newspapers and magazines, stirring imaginations of lost rivers, unidentified bones and jagged formations.

Powell called his new discovery "Fairy Cave." His son, Waldo, purchased Fairy Cave and its surrounding acreage in 1900. After its opening to the public in 1921, Marvel Cave and Fairy Cave competed for the tourist dollar.

Pearl Spurlock wrote in her book that "the caves are entirely different. Each is a wonder within itself. A trip to this section of the country would not be complete without seeing both."

CAVE TOURS AND CHICKEN DINNERS

Waldo Powell's daughters, Hazel and Pansy, were among the first guides in Fairy Cave. Walker Powell, Waldo's son, remembers parking visitors' cars at the cave when he was barely seven years old:

> *When the tours opened in 1921, roads out to the cave were still nothing more than limestone shelves. Most people rode from Branson in taxis to the caves.*
>
> *Opening the gate and asking how many wanted Mama's fried chicken dinner with hot biscuits for a dollar each became my first job. Then, while my sisters toured folks through the cave, I helped Mama wring the chickens' necks and pluck their feathers. She fried them up. Sometimes, as many as ten people gathered around our family's dinner table. In the Depression years, when pennies were precious, we made good money on tour tickets and chicken dinners.*

From 1921 until 1928, tours traversed wooden steps and walkways, which rotted quickly due to the wet and humid nature of the cave. By 1929, steel-reinforced concrete steps and walkways were installed. Raw materials were lowered in buckets to the bottom of the cave. Workers mixed water from the small cave pool with other materials to make the concrete, which was poured into wooden forms. With only slight modifications, the same steps are used today.

The cave is a monument to Waldo Powell, the man whose foresight and ingenuity made it accessible to thousands of visitors. He gained state recognition for his knowledge and work in the field of conservation. Through his efforts, the cave is surrounded by a four-hundred-acre nature preserve. At least ten caves are scattered throughout the property.

In 1969, Silver Dollar City Corporation (now Herschend Family Entertainment Corporation) purchased Fairy Cave from the Powells. Drawing on Truman S. Powell's remarks that the rocks spoke to him, the company renamed the cave Talking Rocks Caverns.

Chapter 2

Shepherd of the Hills

The Ozarks Story

Sitting on Inspiration Point and looking out over the valley is as inspirational as its name. I am drawn to this place—the story—what it means to the area. Shepherd of the Hills Homestead is magic.

—Keith Thurman, director, The Shepherd of the Hills

The fabric of Branson's entertainment history is stitched with men and women who came into the Ozark hills and fused their individual destinies with hill folks and the land itself. Each carried different dreams, desires or needs. The Lynch family sought fortune in the depths of Marvel Cave. S. Fred Prince intended to homestead and research the mountains' native ferns and flowers. And Harold Bell Wright, a Kansas minister who had been diagnosed with consumption, came to breathe the wholesome mountain air.

Due to flooding on the White River, Wright climbed atop a ridge and asked for shelter with John Ross and family—intending to stay only overnight. In keeping with the customs of the Ozarks, Ross and his wife, Georgianna, and their son, Matt, welcomed him to their home. Wright stayed for eight summers.

The Ross cabin had originally been one room. However, due to the production of their steam-powered gristmill and lumber mill, John and his wife (who answered to Anna) were well off financially compared to their Ozarks neighbors. An annual income of $350 and lumber from their own sawmill enlarged their cabin. They had the luxury of a sewing machine for tiny Anna and a push-style lawnmower for tall, brawny John.

Old Matt's Cabin at Shepherd of the Hills Homestead. *Courtesy of Lee Smith.*

Wright eventually pitched a tent on the Ross homestead, making himself a summer home on what would one day be known as Inspiration Point. During winter months, he moved into the cabin, warmed by the old stone fireplace. Over several years, Wright made notes of his adopted Ozarks family, their neighbors and the customs and traditions of mountain culture. He roamed hills and valleys, storing in his imagination scenes for *The Shepherd of the Hills*, a novel published in 1907. His tale hinges on the Ozarks' pioneers and the stranger who entered their simple mountain community. Yet a story comes to life only with conflict. Wright, a master storyteller, delved beneath the masks of peaceful existence to expose the stranger's mysterious past and a father's bitterness over the tragic loss of his only daughter. Mixing facts and traditions with fiction, he wove a spellbinding tale around a strapping young pioneer's silent love for the community's favorite lass, her longing to become a refined lady and the ghostlike boy who roamed the hillsides stirring, superstitious minds with visions of "haints" (an Ozarks name for supernatural spirits).

Wright created tension between the frightening Bald Knobbers and the upstanding citizens who gathered at the old gristmill to picnic, dance and gossip. A country boy turned city slicker pursued the hand of the comely miss. Troublemakers incited fistfights, and masked horsemen torched a cabin. *The Shepherd of the Hills*, a classic story of good versus evil, immediately became a bestseller.

His characters Old Matt, Young Matt and Aunt Mollie—inspired by the Ross family—turned into legends set against the backdrop of oaks and green cedars spreading like a lush blanket over the mountainsides. Many speculated on the identities of Wright's other beloved characters: Sammy Lane, the Old Shepherd, Wash Gibbs, Ollie Stewart, Preachin' Bill and Fiddlin' Jake. However, the author claimed that Uncle Ike, the old postmaster in his story, happened to be the only actual portrayal of a living person, Levi Morrill. His post office stood on the "Trail Nobody Knows How Old." All others, Wright said, including Old Matt and Aunt Mollie, were his created characters.

During his stay in the Ozarks, Wright visited Marble Cave and befriended the Lynch family. He once wrote in a letter to Miriam Lynch that "Marble Cave was the only cave I had in mind when I wrote *The Shepherd of the Hills*." Wright had discovered a small cabin that William Lynch had built inside the cave as his own respite from daily responsibilities—a private "office," so to speak. The idea filtered into Wright's story as the unknown abode of the simple-minded boy, Little Pete, and his father, Howard.

THE STORY TOOK ON ITS OWN LIFE

Within a year of *The Shepherd of the Hills*'s publication, the world beat a path to the Ozarks, eager to view up close Wright's picturesque pocket of earth and its peculiar populace—seemingly set apart from the outside world. At that time, Ozarks manners mandated that a host invite people in for a meal—or to spend the night. Dozens of people converged on the Ross homestead. Crowds of curious strangers literally ate the family out of house and home. Rather than violate their rules of hospitality, they moved in 1910 across Roark Valley to Garber, Missouri, and opened a general store.

With the property vacant, visitors took away pieces of the wood siding from the old barn and stones from the fireplace and foundation of the cabin. Souvenir-seeking tourists practically dismantled the old mill—pocketing bolts, nuts and bits of the structure. Within three years, the Rosses sold their homestead to M.R. Driver, who added a screened room on the north side and turned "Old Matt's Cabin" into a wayside inn for tourist dining. In the 1913 season, about seven hundred people took meals at the homestead. John and Anna Ross lived ten more years at Garber, running their store and a post office. They both died in 1923. By that time, their son had moved to California. After his parents' deaths, he sold all of the furnishings and personal belongings related to the old cabin or to Harold Bell Wright. The prototype for Young Matt died on the West Coast in 1934.

MISS LIZZIE

By October 1926, M.R. Driver sold the homestead to a Springfield banker, Horace Dewitt McDaniel, who deeded the property four months later to his daughter, Lizzie McDaniel, an educated schoolteacher and socialite in Springfield. Miss Lizzie, as she became affectionately known to hill folks, recognized the importance of preserving the homestead for its key role in the widely read novel—as well as for the lore of the Ozarks. Between 1927 and 1929, McDaniel staged two-act plays that reenacted *The Shepherd of the Hills* on the lawn of the Ross cabin. Tourist interest continuously grew.

In 1934, McDaniel granted a right of way to the State of Missouri for the purpose of building today's well-known Highway 76 through the homestead. Two years later, she executed a fifty-year lease to Missouri for 6.86 acres within the homestead to "develop and beautify a scenic turnout on Inspiration Hill." The leased acreage included the Ross cabin, which, by that time, was commonly named Old Matt's Cabin.

At the outset, McDaniel lived in the cabin and traveled across the Ozarks on the back of a mule, buying back all the items that Charles Ross had auctioned. A well-to-do woman who had been at the center of social and

Antique desk that once belonged to the Ross family, now on display in Old Matt's Cabin. *Courtesy of Lee Smith.*

civic affairs in Springfield, she often wore Paris fashions yet she blended with the culture of mountain people, speaking their language—including cursing when a situation provoked her.

In 1936, McDaniel built her house on the north slope of Boulder Bald. From a family home in Springfield, she salvaged the solid mahogany staircase and fireplace mantel, along with cornices, marble, doors and windows. Stones from the property and lumber from its trees went into the foundation and walls of the spacious home with vaulted ceilings. Today, the structure serves as the ticket office for Shepherd of the Hills Homestead.

Inside the cabin, open for guided tours today, McDaniel's saddle hangs on the back porch alongside one used by Anna Ross. A ceiling lamp in the living room once hung in Harold Bell Wright's tent, pitched on the lawn. A spinning wheel and a weasel for making skeins of yarn both sit by the old stone fireplace. Various kitchen tools and Anna Ross's size-four shoes are displayed. Through the diligence of Lizzie McDaniel and her dedication to preserve a long-ago setting, the home for the Ross family and the Kansas preacher who made the Ozarks famous stands as the centerpiece of the Shepherd of the Hills Homestead.

CHANGING HANDS

When McDaniel died in 1946, she bequeathed the homestead to her brother, H.B. McDaniel. Three months later, he sold the homestead to the Branson Civic League. Within another three months, the civic league sold most of the homestead to Dr. Bruce and Mary Trimble. However, the civic league maintained ownership of Inspiration Point and the cabin. Until 1966, when the title was transferred to the Trimbles, the owners paid a fee to the library club in the name of the civic league for the use of the cabin and Inspiration Point. Once again, a family entertained families in the Ozarks. By 1950, tourism rebounded. The Trimbles converted Lizzie McDaniel's home into a second museum on the homestead.

Dr. Trimble had long dreamed of an outdoor theater in the Ozarks. Upon his death, the story of Marvel Cave's development repeated itself—a widow and children carried the dream forward. Mary Trimble, her son Mark and his wife Lea became the driving force in the direction and future of the homestead. The Trimbles owned Shepherd of the Hills Homestead between 1946 and 1986.

THE SHEPHERD OF THE HILLS

Keith Thurman, current director of the *Shepherd of the Hills* drama at the homestead's amphitheater, recalls that the drama in two acts continued on Inspiration Point until the 1940s. "In the 1950s, the play went to Taneycomo's lakefront in downtown Branson," he says. "College drama students from Southern Illinois University and Southwest Missouri State College (now Missouri State University) performed the roles. The first script, which burned in a dressing room fire, involved Young Matt carrying a stove rather than lifting a steam engine."

Thurman remembers that the production moved to Beacon Hill Theater at School of the Ozarks. "In 1960, Mark Trimble decided the time was right to produce the drama at the homestead and make his father's dream come true," he continues. "Working with Jim Collie as scriptwriter and director, and Shad Heller as casting director, they formed the Old Mill Players, Inc. They produced the first *Shepherd of the Hills* outdoor drama on August 6, 1960, in the newly built amphitheater at the site of John Ross's old mill. The amphitheater had an initial capacity of 275 seats."

Thurman notes that in the early days the directors consciously cast local residents in the roles that fit personalities and body type. They specifically advertised that performers were hill folks—possibly re-creating the most important event in their history.

In 1966, Mark Trimble bought out the other members of Old Mill Player's, Inc. and increased marketing. Attendance grew. The theater expanded and ultimately accommodated almost three thousand guests. Also in 1966, the title to the property retained by the Branson Civic League reverted to the Trimble family.

Shepherd of the Hills
Homestead entrance,
Inspiration Tower
in the background.
Courtesy of Lee Smith.

A COACH BECOMES WASH GIBBS

In 1965, Gary Snaden took the coaching job at the Branson High School and moved his family to Branson. "I had played football in college, and the *Shepherd of the Hills* director looked me over and thought I could take the hits in a fistfight," says Snaden. "I had never acted, but when he told me the role of Wash Gibbs paid $17.50 a night, I asked, 'Where do I show up?' That was a lot of money in 1966."

"I had no idea that I would one day take a big step to buy the property," he continues. "However, *Shepherd of the Hills* gets into your blood."

Twenty years after stepping onto that set as Wash Gibbs, Gary Snaden and his wife, Pat, took ownership of the historic property. The tradition of families entertaining families continued.

"But it's more than our family," Pat explains. "We have ninety actors in the drama and approximately three hundred total employees—people who drive the Jeeps, work in the shops, do landscaping, sell tickets. We all feel like family. One woman has been an usher and square dancer in the drama for forty years."

Pat notes that some individuals outgrow their roles. "Actor Terry Sanders's son, Austin, started playing Little Pete almost ten years ago. Now he does sound and lights," she says. "Terry's whole family performs in the production. He alternates the roles of Ollie Stewart and Doc Coughlin. Dede Sanders plays Mrs. Wheeler, the woman who henpecks her husband. Their younger son, Evan, is in his sixth season as Little Pete."

"The roles are scripted, but each actor has his or her own

Greg Winters as Doc Coughlin and Terry Sanders as Ollie Stewart in *Shepherd of the Hills*. *Courtesy of Terry Sanders.*

mannerisms and ad libs," Pat continues. "One of the Ollie Stewarts runs and hugs a tree and looks like a tree frog. They all have gimmicks and tricks that keep the show fresh."

FISTFIGHTS ARE REAL

Gary says that the fistfights today are choreographed. "Every actor knows exactly where and how to fall," he adds. "But when I played Wash Gibbs, we had to project—no wireless microphones. We actually hit the other actor, at least with an open hand, to make the sound of a slap."

"We had broken collar bones, teeth knocked out and bloody noses," he continues. "I knocked Young Matt out one night, and for a few moments, it looked as though Wash Gibbs was going to win the fight. Young Matt came to just in time."

THE STORY OF THE OZARKS ENDURES

Over the years, Keith Thurman has rewritten the script three times, condensing the show and eliminating dragging dialogue. "The 1960 script ran two hours and forty-five minutes," he says. "Today's show is one hour and fifty-five minutes with an intermission. I try to have action every three to four minutes."

In the first script, Aunt Mollie told the story. Thurman switched the viewpoint to the Old Shepherd and removed swear words, although they are in the book. "In 1900, if Harold Bell Wright had written the book in the language of the Ozarks as it was spoken, there would have been more swear words," Thurman says. "Hill folks were Christian, God-fearing people, but they did use foul language."

"We realistically tell the story," he says. "Every line of dialogue comes from the book. However, we've added more explanation of the plot in the beginning because fewer people in the audience today have read the book."

"With all the glitz, glitter and gizmos now, it's hard to entertain a crowd," Thurman adds. "Still, I believe folks are returning to a good story line. And this story is magic. The characters talk as folks did before 1900. They fight and torch a cabin. Riders thunder through the set on horseback, shooting full-load blanks from their pistols. Wagons pulled by draft horses rattle into the party scene. A vintage 1908 DeWitt automobile sputters into the drama.

Right: Torching of the Old Shepherd's cabin in *Shepherd of the Hills*. *Courtesy of Terry Sanders.*

Below: Gunfight in *Shepherd of the Hills*. *Courtesy of Terry Sanders.*

Young Matt actually lifts a steam engine. True love and a struggle for power play out against a darkened Ozarks sky. The story builds with emotion as we re-create Branson in the late 1800s."

When the Snadens bought the property in 1986, they focused on making the most of the buildings and amenities for daytime tours, as well as the nightly plays. Today, Jeep-drawn trams carry guests around the homestead. A guide narrates the property's history and heritage, including Old Matt's Cabin (listed on the National Historic Registry). At Inspiration Point, a monument marks the spot where author Harold Bell Wright camped while compiling his notes for *The Shepherd of the Hills*.

Weathered statues of six of the main characters in Wright's story stand on Inspiration Point, the second-highest peak in Missouri. Yet guests can zoom 230 feet higher in a streamlined elevator to the top of Inspiration Tower, built in 1989 by the Snadens. From the tower's height, views stretch over Mutton Hollow and the hills of northern Arkansas.

In 1991, the Snadens saved the Morgan Community Church from demolition and moved the aging structure, its furnishings and the inscribed cornerstone to Inspiration Point. The tidy white clapboard house of worship is similar to the churches that Harold Bell Wright ministered in as he traveled across southern Missouri.

EXPANDING ENTERTAINMENT

More than a century ago, copies of *The Shepherd of the Hills* passed through the mail at the old Notch Post Office, going out to readers across the nation. Tourists came to see the setting of the novel. Today, families still travel to Branson to relive the story of the Ozarks—returning with grandchildren and great-grandchildren.

"We keep the integrity of the drama, adding only some special effects but never changing the story," Gary Snaden says. "However, we have a new generation to entertain. We improve our facilities with attractions such as the Inspiration Tower. At Christmas, which has become one of Branson's busiest seasons, Pat puts a red bow and a string of lights on everything on the grounds. She started animated displays, and now we have two and a half miles of lighted scenes called 'Trail of Lights.'"

In 2010, the Snadens added "Vigilante," a zip line allowing visitors to step off a platform at the top of Inspiration Tower and literally whoosh over the treetops to another point on the homestead.

AN OZARKS TRADITION

The Shepherd of the Hills marked a turning point in Harold Bell Wright's literary career. The book's success also marked a milestone in the Branson story. Starting with John and Anna Ross, who opened their home to strangers, and continuing with families and individuals such as Lizzie McDaniel, the Trimbles and now the Snadens, families still entertain other families in the Ozarks tradition.

CHAPTER 3

A CHICAGO FAMILY AFFECTS
THE OZARKS

That gaping sinkhole leading to Marvel Cave forever linked William Lynch and Hugo Herschend, an adventurous Danish immigrant. Ironically, the men never met. However, their individual grit set the stage for the start of Silver Dollar City, an entertainment flagship that influenced the destiny of tourism in the Missouri Ozarks.

When Hugo and Mary Herschend, a blended Chicago family with two teenage sons, vacationed in the Ozarks in the 1940s, they stayed in a housekeeping cabin built by William Lynch. By 1949, cave work had become too strenuous for Miriam and Genevieve Lynch. Hugo Herschend, captivated by the beauty of the Ozarks, considered the tour cave as a retirement business. He leased the property, planning that Mary would manage the cave during the summers, while he continued to support their family as a representative for Electrolux Vacuum Company in Chicago.

"I didn't understand why my mother cried as we left Chicago that summer in 1950," Pete Herschend says. "To me and my brother, Jack, summer jobs at a cave surpassed the tales of Tom Sawyer and Huck Finn. We were the only boys in our neighborhood whose family operated a cave!"

Jack Herschend, a new high school graduate, admits that he and Pete had not a single business thought in their heads. "To a seventeen-year-old, cave guide Fannabelle Nickel was the greatest gal I'd ever met," he says. "She took Pete and me exploring almost every night, showing us miles of this underground wonder. Soon, despite our mother's anxiety, we led exploring parties and tourists through the cave on our own."

Hugo and Mary Herschend with Mary's niece, Pat Green, at the ticket desk for Marvel Cave. *Courtesy of Silver Dollar City Archives.*

Early tour of Marvel Cave after the Herschends leased the property and made improvements. *Courtesy of Silver Dollar City Archives.*

According to Jack, Pete quickly mastered tall tales, often urging his guests to reset their watches to "Stone County Time." He spun a long story about why it was important to set their time ahead a half hour on the odd hours and forty-five minutes on the even hours.

The first summer of their leased operation, the Herschends welcomed eight thousand guests. The three Ozarks men, Lester Vining, Rex Johnson and Bert Lewallen—who had worked for the Lynch sisters—stayed on with the Herschends. Under Hugo's plan for improvements, they installed electric lights and replaced the rickety walkways with concrete paths.

"The ingredients for an exciting life were here," Jack says. "In the 1950s, the outside world had passed over the Ozarks, leaving a primitive way of life—no electricity, no indoor plumbing and water trucked in from Reeds Spring. For eight years, we operated with no telephone!"

The family bought an additional 640 acres surrounding the cave. Betty Rantz recalls that they moved into a little house on the property, one that she figures her dad had covered with the green siding. "The only time I ever heard my father speak disrespectfully about Mary Herschend, calling her 'that durn-fool woman,' happened when she asked Dad to install a toilet inside her makeshift living quarters that also housed the cave's ticket office and the employee lounge," she says. As a condition for moving to the Ozarks, Mary Herschend insisted on indoor plumbing. Her neighbors said she was "puttin' on airs!"

"I remember Daddy saying, 'I tried to tell her we just don't do that inside our houses; it's not *nice!*'" With a laugh, Rantz says that her father probably could not call up the word "sanitary."

"He installed the toilet, and soon after, he put one in our house over on Compton Ridge," Rantz adds.

Creative Marketing

In the meantime, Hugo Herschend applied his marketing skills to the promotion of his tourist attraction. During the 1950s, live radio broadcasts and annual square dance festivals staged in the large auditorium room made headlines in local and big city newspapers. Advertisements on billboards and in radio blurbs touted the cave's natural air conditioning. Decades before, S. Fred Prince had written in his description of the Cathedral Room: "The acoustics are so perfect that conversation in a moderate voice at one end may be distinctly understood at the other, yet the crash of a large band is mellowed and sweetened. There is practically no echo."

Hugo Herschend capitalized on his natural auditorium, and visitors returned year after year to sit on benches installed on the sloping rock wall above the Cathedral Room floor. Over a three-day weekend, they watched ladies in swirling skirts and gents in scuffed boots square-dance to a caller's cadenced voice and a country band—all in an unspoiled underground setting.

"Pete came up with the idea of having the first underground radio broadcast," Jack says. "We dragged radio equipment across the lakes inside the cave, using the inflatable raft our parents had given us for a Christmas present. We explored places no human had ever been and broadcast a radio program that went to Tokyo, Berlin and around the world. Pete, like his dad Hugo, was brilliant about getting out the story of Marvel Cave."

"In our small operation, everybody had several jobs," Jack continues. "Fannabelle, Rex, Lester and Bert were cave guides, sign painters, construction and maintenance crew and landscapers."

"We had no money for marketing," he notes. "Fannabelle taught me to paint signs. From the woods, I cut cedar poles and painted lettering on sheets of Masonite. I could put up a sign for $18.75."

Every person who worked at Marvel Cave, or later at Silver Dollar City, either experienced firsthand or knew a story about Mary Herschend firing someone, including Jack. "My mother had excellent taste. She knew what she wanted," Jack says. "But she could not read a blueprint or visualize from a sketch.

"Once when Rex, Bert, Lester and I were putting up an entrance sign for Marvel Cave, we used some old twelve-by-twelve timbers, thirty-five feet

Marvel Cave Park entrance sign. *Courtesy of Silver Dollar City Archives.*

long," he says. "Two of the timbers went down five feet into the ground to stand thirty feet tall. We notched the third one to go across the top and hold up the sign."

"We had no equipment, so the four of us balanced on ladders and pushed up the eight-hundred-pound beam," he goes on. "Very dangerous, now that I look back on it. We seated it. Mary came out, looked over our work and said, 'It's about four feet too high.'"

"I said, 'Mary, we've risked life and limb, and we're not taking it down.' She fired me. I never went away, but she didn't talk to me for about ninety days!"

Jack Herschend's Passion for Marvel Cave

When the time came for Jack to enroll in college following that first summer of cave management, he had decided to make a career out of the opportunities he saw around Marvel Cave.

"I told my dad there were cement stairs to build, lights to string and highway signs to paint," Jack recalls. "Marvel Cave was a 'get-by-the-skin-of-your-teeth' operation. I saw no sense in my leaving the business for schooling."

After long evenings trying to convince his son of the importance of higher education, Hugo Herschend relented. He assigned Jack the job of carrying sacks of cement for the replacement steps to the waterfall in the cave.

"Starting in September, I carried ninety-four-pound sacks, one on each shoulder, down 505 vertical feet. Free of that load, I seemed to float back up the wooden scaffolding," Jack says. "By Christmas, college made sense!"

He enrolled at Northwestern University near their Illinois home and completed his degree in three and a half years. "I never regretted those months of work because they gave me a clear focus on the broad business education I needed to run our family business."

During the summers of his college years, the wiry son of Mary Herschend returned to the Ozarks, guided in the cave and helped with operations. He admits "falling in love" with Fannabelle Nickel before he met her daughter, Sherry. "Fannabelle was a high-energy fifty-year-old who always had a play party, a horseback ride to the river or a cave exploration planned," Jack explains. "She was typical of the kind of people working for the Lynch sisters."

He goes on to say that Sherry and her mother were "cut from the same cloth." Having grown up around Marvel Cave, Sherry often danced on the two- by four-inch railing around the platform high above the cave's entrance. Guests stood amazed, but Jack was smitten.

In 1954, Jack graduated from college, received his ROTC commission as a second lieutenant in the U.S. Marine Corps and married the animated Sherry Nickel in the Cathedral Room, aglow with thousands of candles.

After the Herschends' wedding and Jack's assignment with the Marine Corps, the couple returned to the Ozarks. Sherry sold tickets for the cave tours and hung the baskets of flowers outside on posts. Sometimes, she slipped away from the office when Jack guided a tour and crept through the darkness to appear at the bottom of the Waterfall Room, where the group turned to climb back out.

"My hair was brown at the time," Jack says with a smile. "It turned white from Sherry sneaking up in the darkness of the cave's depth and scaring me—and the tourists!"

Marvel Cave continued to be Jack's avocation. He thrived on strapping on a backpack and climbing rope ladders to explore unknown passages. Often on three-day excursions, he hiked, crawled and climbed to distant chambers in which an underground river flows into two lakes.

Over the years, as Silver Dollar City developed above the great cavern, he became knowledgeable as a spelunker. The National Cave Association elected him as president. Clients as far away as Puerto Rico's commonwealth government sought his expertise as an explorer-consultant.

THE IMPOSSIBLE CABLE TRAIN

Hugo Herschend's vision for improvements included a European-style cable car system to transport visitors out of the cave. Before he could initiate his plans, a fatal heart attack snuffed out his life at age fifty-five.

"I remember my mother, grief-stricken and lacking in entrepreneurial skills, questioning my dad's legacy in Missouri's deepest cave," Jack says. "Nevertheless, with self-discipline cultivated on an Illinois farm, she cut her ties in Chicago and never looked back!"

A year after Hugo's death in 1955, the cave train project began in earnest, with Jack in charge. Years before, Fannabelle had led Pete and Jack to the formation called Blondie's Throne—named for Charles Smallwood, who was lost in the cave in the late 1800s. Rescuers found the boy sleeping near this formation, his blond hair gleaming in the candlelight.

"When Pete and I discovered Blondie's Throne, we knew we weren't far from the surface," Jack says. "We wanted to get to the top. We talked our parents into giving us an aluminum extension ladder for Christmas. An unusual gift, but that's how we discovered the area where the train comes in now."

"After returning home in 1957, Sherry and I heard complaints from guests about climbing five hundred vertical feet out of the cave after a tour," he continues. "We determined it was time to follow through on Dad's plan."

An engineer surveyed the cave, laying it out on the surface. "It didn't look accurate to me, so we asked our uncle, Jake Rinker, to do another survey. He missed the top of Blondie's Throne by 11 feet. The engineer had missed it by 150 feet."

"At that time, my mother had borrowed $18,000—her limit at the local bank," Jack says. "That money had to dig the tunnel, put in the walkways and lights from the Waterfall to Blondie's Throne and then put in the cable train. If we had gone with the engineer's survey, $18,000 would have gone in a hole to nowhere."

Cable train owners in Chattanooga, Tennessee, told Jack that there was no possible way to run such a train around the 157-degree curve in Marvel Cave. "Next, I met with engineers in Joplin who confirmed that it could not be done," Jack says. "Bert Lewallen, Lester Vining and Rex Johnson had all been to the Oregon logging woods. They were not highly educated men, but in terms of experience, they were outstanding."

"Bert remembered snaking trees out of the West Coast forests using convex wheels that thread a cable. Those three men, over a half-hour lunch break, figured out how we could go this way and that way using twenty-seven wheels to pull a cable train," Jack continues. "Creative thinking on their part built the train. For six months, six days a week, we came in shifts to dig and blast. The three men came early and drilled four-foot-deep holes. I was the powder monkey and came in later to blast one stick of dynamite at a time. We'd allow overnight for the fumes to dissipate."

Jack remembers stretching their borrowed money with used materials. "We had setbacks," he says. "In 1957, after we had everything ready to go, a downpour of rain filled up the tunnel with clay. Water ran over the hand railing and Blondie's Throne. We lost the whole season. In 1958, we dug out all the clay."

Jack boarded the train for its initial trial run into the cave, unaware that the used $7/8$-inch cable spliced to a $5/8$-inch cable was unclamped. Racing unrestrained at about sixty-seven miles per hour in two and a half seconds,

The "impossible" cable train at Marvel Cave. *Courtesy of Lee Smith.*

the fearless Jack hit a rock wall. He broke his leg in five places, had to have fifty-seven stitches in his head and crushed three disks in his spine. But he lived. The train, its cable hooked and tested properly, started operation, with Casey Jones Jr. as the conductor on its first run. The first year of operation, Marvel Cave's business increased 40 percent. The train continues to transport guests safely from the cave's depths.

SETTING A RECORD

On July 7, 1963, Don Piccard, credited as the father of modern sport hot air ballooning, lifted his balloon and set the world's underground altitude record in the Cathedral Room of Marvel Cave. Four months prior, he had made the first successful crossing of the English Channel in a hot air balloon. No doubt, this commemorative day inspired Jack and Sherry Herschend's son, Jim, to become a balloonist. In 1987 and 1988, Jim Herschend and attorney Carson Elliff piloted two hot air balloons in the expansive entrance room. Both men had been guides in Marvel Cave during the 1970s.

In 1988, businesswoman Becky Petrehn stood atop one balloon, enabling her to be the first person to touch the ceiling of the Cathedral Room. In 1994, five hot air balloons were flown simultaneously to celebrate the cave's 100th anniversary of guided tours.

THE DREAM OF TWO MEN FULFILLED BY THEIR FAMILIES

The Herschends acknowledge that their award-winning theme park surrounding Marvel Cave's entrance exists because of a mysterious calling within both William Lynch and Hugo Herschend. Two families focused on a dream of the men they loved. With hard work, prayer, deep faith and the help of Ozarks strangers who became friends, they changed the face of Roark Mountain forever. The legacy of two men and one cave lives on for present and future generations in a thriving Silver Dollar City.

Upon their deaths, Miriam and Genevieve Lynch bequeathed the cave property to the College of the Ozarks and the Branson Presbyterian Church. The United States Department of the Interior proclaimed Marvel Cave to be a Natural Landmark. Silver Dollar City includes a tour of Marvel Cave with its admission price.

CHAPTER 4

A SILVER DOLLAR
NAMES A CITY

I see the Silver Dollar City founders as a beautiful grandfather clock. Pete represents the face—the visible scenes of the city. Jack is on the inside, making things work. And Mary is the hands. She set the time.

—Edd Akers, former Silver Dollar City employee

Silver Dollar City is a once-upon-a-time place, built from the buried foundations of a vanished village called Marmaros. "One day in 1954, an eighty-year-old traveling salesman named Charlie Sullivan pulled up to Marvel Cave Park in a 1937 Buick," recalls cofounder Jack Herschend. "He said he was born in the town and had lived in the back of the general store for seven years. In the woods, he kicked aside brambles and briars to show me remnants of stone foundations for the hotel, the general store and the house where Dr. Jones lived. He even told us where to dig for the doctor's well."

At Galena, Missouri, Jack discovered that indeed there had been a bustling village where folks traded goods, sold supplies to miners and even schooled their young. The idea to rebuild the village stirred Mary Herschend's imagination.

Jack says. "As the tour business grew, Mary had noticed that often the mother waited topside, perhaps with babies, while the father took several older children in the cave. Also, the tour was too strenuous for expectant mothers or people with heart problems. With the goal of making a trip to Marvel Cave more enjoyable for all guests, we tossed around plans to rebuild some of the old structures."

In 1959, the Herschends and their Ozarks workforce built a tower from the Marvel Cave sinkhole to the top of the debris pile, creating steps down to the Cathedral Room. The cable train now chugged up the tunnel, carrying passengers from the cave's depths. That winter, prior to the 1960 season, the family turned their attention to new buildings that looked old. Mary Herschend supervised. Jack carried the hammer and ruler.

Russ Pearson had arrived on the Marvel Cave scene, and he designed and created one-eighth scale models for the village. "However, the showman in Russ suggested buildings with false fronts and cardboard effects. Mary said, 'No!'"

"From the beginning, Mary committed to authenticity and preservation," Jack says. "Above all, she refused to allow trees to be destroyed in the building process. As a result, the shops around the Town Square turned into curious shapes with notched porches."

The hammer marks of both Jack and Pete, along with the make-do ingenuity and practical skills of their native Ozarks crew, remain on the storefronts today. "We—our family from Chicago—were blessed to discover the Ozarks can-do mindset," Jack says. "Those hill folk, not braggadocios, had the attitude that they could do anything. Whether putting a cable train in the cave, a tower to the Cathedral Room or rebuilding the old mining town, they'd figure out how to do it and stretch every borrowed nickel."

HOMECOMING FOR PETE

Following Hugo Herschend's death, Jack or Pete continuously remained on the property to help their mother. Pete stayed out of college, while Jack fulfilled his military duty.

"After Jack came home, I went to college in 1956, graduated in 1958 and finished my military service in 1960," Pete recalls. "Since Jack was devoted to the Missouri business, I planned a career elsewhere."

However, the returning army man's plans changed when a contingent of employees from the new Silver Dollar City, most of them wearing six-shooters slung over their hips, met him on the tarmac at the Springfield Airport. "The next day at the property, I discovered a blacksmith shop, a jail, the print shop, an ice cream parlor and a store integrated into the woods on one side of our parking lot. Tucked behind the General Store was the one paying attraction, 'Slantin' Sam's Ole Miner's Shack,' a building that throws everything out of balance," Pete says.

One of Silver Dollar City's first attractions: an authentic stagecoach driven by Jerry Stang. Standing, *left to right*, are Jack, Mary and Pete Herschend. *Courtesy of Silver Dollar City Archives.*

Between the Wilderness Church and the mysterious spring at the top of the hill, Jerry Stang ran the other paying attraction, an authentic stagecoach pulled by sturdy draft horses. Beside the Wilderness Church, half of the McHaffie Homestead had been reconstructed.

Jack and Mary Herschend thought that they were building a replica of the 1880s town so folks unable to take the cave tour would have something to do. When 125,000 people came to Silver Dollar City that first year, they realized that they had a themed entertainment business.

Pete notes the gifts to Silver Dollar City, beginning with Marvel Cave, an attraction that had drawn eighty thousand guests in 1959. "In 1960, the publicity for Table Rock Lake brought people into the region," he says. "Another basic tool helped advance Silver Dollar City—a good map of Branson on the backside of our brochure. Visitors carried that map around in their pockets."

"We credit the name of our mountain village to Don Richardson, a former scriptwriter for Springfield's *Ozark Jubilee* who became our public relations/marketing department," Pete continues. "We had no money for advertising, so Don believed that if we gave change in silver dollars, guests would pay for gas and meals using that relatively uncommon piece of currency. His theory worked. Before long, waitresses, store clerks and gas station attendants were stating: 'You've been to Silver Dollar City!'"

Pete recalls that Russ Pearson also designed several shows to entertain guests. "We stole the theme of the Hatfield/McCoy feud and built street skits around the story of Zeke Hatfield and Sarey Ellen McCoy—two

Delivery of silver dollars to Silver Dollar City. *Courtesy of Silver Dollar City Archives.*

A feud between the Hatfields and McCoys on Silver Dollar City's Main Street. *Courtesy of Silver Dollar City Archives.*

young lovers forbidden to cross a line in the street Ma McCoy drew with the toe of her boot," he says. "We couldn't afford entertainers. Our first year, the thirteen people who worked at Silver Dollar City became 'hams' in the skits."

Pete played the role of Zeke Hatfield. Jack mingled the roles of Doc Carmichael and the undertaker who carted Zeke away in a wheelbarrow after an enraged Pa McCoy shot him dead. "It was slapstick, ad-lib comedy,"

Jack says, recalling how the flower tucked in Pete's bib overalls wilted when he expired. "No script, just ordinary people acting out a general plot with key phrases spoken in that natural Ozarks dialect. Our guests loved it."

LOVE SETTLES A FEUD

In Silver Dollar City's third season, JoDee Remien took a summer job as a clerk in the General Store. Three times a day, she dropped everything and entered Main Street as Sarey Ellen McCoy. "When I put on that long dress every morning, I had a free pass for fun, almost like a daylong costume party," she says. "I can still see Colonel Ray, his black pants and vest and his goatee. He represented an 1800s gentleman stepping on the porch of the General Store and calling out to Myrna Escher, this lovely lady in the candy shop—her white hair done up in a bun. That kind of natural banter went on all day between workers and guests."

"I know of no other entertainment place at that time where the employees stepped into a character," JoDee goes on. "I was never told what to say to guests in the park and only to repeat whatever Zeke Hatfield said to me in the street scene."

"Every skit, he gave me something, sometimes a 'fleur,' [Ozarks for flower] or a slim slick sycamore stick," she noted. "At Silver Dollar City, everyone played and pretended."

The old General Store at Silver Dollar City.
Courtesy of Silver Dollar City Archives.

JoDee first held Pete's hand across Ma McCoy's line in the dirt. A romance blossomed, and they were married on June 25, 1966.

"Right out of high school and on my first summer job, I wanted to be like Mary Herschend," JoDee says. She recalls the sale of summer sausages in the General Store. "One day, both finances and stock were low. The other clerks and I got out the last sausage and sliced it," she tells. "We had samples; the guests had samples. Mary came in. She had a sample."

"Then she asked, 'Did the summer sausages come in?' Fortunately, Mary didn't stay long enough to hear our answer," JoDee says, smiling now at the scene. "I wanted to be doing something right when she walked in—or when she heard about it. To me, she had an aura of excitement and romance."

MARY HERSCHEND: LEADING LADY OF MISSOURI TOURISM

Mary Herschend, an educated city housewife widowed at age fifty-six, suddenly became the head of a tour business in a cave that did not claim her affection. In the mid-1950s, a woman in the business world commanded little respect. Added to that fact, Ozarks culture, suspicious of anyone who came from "off," judged her an outsider. Yet she never considered giving up on her husband's dream. She found friendship in the two Lynch sisters who, despite their broad education and cultural upbringing, had lived and worked amicably for fifty years among Ozarks neighbors.

Headstrong at times, Mary demanded the best from her sons and her crew: Bert Lewallen, Fannabelle Nickel, Lester and Lois Vining and Rex Johnson. In the first decade the Herschends leased Marvel Cave, their employees grew to almost a dozen. Jack remembers the time as a hectic, creative episode filled with conflicts of opinions and wills, but with his mother's judgment always being the final decision.

Mary Herschend, founder of Silver Dollar City. *Courtesy of Silver Dollar City Archives.*

He recalls building the stone fireplace in the Hospitality House. Mary looked it over and said, "No, that's not what I had in mind." Jack and his loyal crew took down the stones, hammered away the mortar and rebuilt the massive fireplace. Again, his mother said, "No, that's not what I want."

Jack remembers saying, "Yes, Mary, that *is* what you want. We're not rebuilding it again." She fired him—another of the three occasions during that first decade.

Pete remembers his job as foreman for new construction but *never* as the boss. That role belonged to his mother. Andy Miller, a set designer for *Ozark Jubilee*, had joined their staff. He sided with Mary on realistic 1800s buildings.

"We'd pour the footings for a new structure and be ready to put up the walls when Mary would come out, walk up and down looking at it from every angle, confer with Andy and then decide it wasn't exactly in the right place," he says. "We'd get the sledgehammers, tear it all out and start over. I was exasperated, but looking back, I cannot recall an instance when Mary wasn't right."

Edd Akers, an early employee and currently co-owner of Akers & Arney Insurance Company in Branson, recalls that Mary Herschend also fired him. She quickly rehired him, however, and Edd often drove her to juried art shows around the area. "While she judged arts and crafts, I'd visit a corn shuck doll maker or some other craftsman, constantly seeking people to display and demonstrate their work at Silver Dollar City."

Mary found an old log church along Bear Creek. She had it dismantled, each log numbered and moved to their fledgling Ozarks village. At first, she vetoed the site selected for reconstructing Wilderness Church. A large sycamore stood in that spot. Nevertheless, when Lester Vining offered to hew a pulpit from the great tree's trunk, she agreed.

Akers helped reconstruct the old church. "I've seen people walk inside and suddenly grow quiet, realizing they were in a place to revere," he says. "The view from the large window behind the tree trunk pulpit overlooks the same hills that inspired Harold Bell Wright back in the late 1800s."

A native of the Ozarks, Akers concurs that hill people were slow to accept outsiders. "But if they saw goodness, if they encountered people who didn't have the 'smarts' of hill folks but knew how to get along with others, they took them in," he says. "The Herschends credited the gifts they recognized in each person. They listened—and learned. They would do anything for their crew, and in turn, those early workers would do anything for them."

Branson and the surrounding region took note of Mary Herschend and the contributions her rising company made to the tourism industry of the area. She was invited to serve on the board of directors of the Ozark

Playground Association and the Branson Chamber of Commerce. She joined the chambers of commerce in neighboring towns. In 1968, the Federal Small Business Administration honored her as Missouri Small Businessman of the Year (note the honor for business*man*).

At the First Annual Governor's Conference on Tourism, Mary Herschend received the 1972 Missouri Tourism Award. The Springfield Chamber of Commerce conferred a similar award. She also received the Two Marys Award, created by the Branson Chamber of Commerce in recognition of the achievements of Mary Herschend and Mary Trimble—a widow who also picked up her husband's dream and guided development of the Shepherd of the Hills Homestead.

Reverend Bob Deeds at the pulpit hewn by Lester Vining for Wilderness Church, Silver Dollar City. *Courtesy of Arline Chandler.*

Mary Herschend died in 1983. Over thirty-four years, she had gained status among Ozarks folks. More importantly, the Missouri House of Representatives distinguished her in a resolution stating, "the House recognizes in the life and works of Mary Rinker Herschend those attributes which characterize and define a true Missouri pioneer…who helped create a wave of recreational development which greatly contributed to the rise of tourism as one of Missouri's top industries."

A Train Whistles into the City

Jack Herschend delights in telling the story of his brother buying their steam train from the Henry Ford family. "He proudly brought home a hunk of junk that looked like a steam train," Jack says, adding that Pete bought track and services of an engineer, Ty Smith. "We laid the track and tested the train on a trial run, naming the ride the Frisco–Silver Dollar Line."

The Frisco–Silver Dollar Line steams into the city. *Courtesy of Silver Dollar City Archives.*

"Pete had been told the train would climb a 5 percent grade," Jack continues. "But we had an 11 percent downhill grade, and the train was flying forty miles per hour with the brakes on. The engineer leaped off. Fortunately, the iron monster did not jump track—but it took months for me to forgive Pete!"

Problems persisted. Through the first year, the train's flues leaked. Every Friday night, the ride closed early to let the firebox cool—at least to one hundred degrees. Pete greased up the smallest person on staff, which happened to be Jack, and he stuck one arm at a time into the steaming box to remove charred residue.

Out of those ashes rose the classic train robbery. Few guests today know that in the early days, the train had to build up a head of steam to make it up a hill and back to the depot. An inventive robbery, staged by college boys playing the notorious Civil War bushwhacker Alf Bolin and gang, stopped the train long enough for the engineer to shovel coal into the firebox. A short whistle signaled that the boiler had steam. Entertained guests were none the wiser.

Today, Jack and Pete laugh about pouring sand on the tracks on a wet, dewy day so the train wheels would have traction climbing the hill. They also remember that the train sucked coal through the flue and threw hot cinders into the woods. They stationed small guys with wet gunnysacks along the route to grab the embers.

"In the first years, the train broke down a lot," Jack says. "We had no roundhouse. We pulled out a few railroad ties, dug a pit, and Bert Lewallen took a few wrenches and hammered the gears back in place. He was one gifted man."

Pete says in retrospect that lack of capital limited them in building Silver Dollar City. "But if we had had money to duplicate what is here today, we would not have been able to grow the Silver Dollar City family and its culture. The learning curve in the 1960s was the best training in how to make a business work. The heart of this company lies in the people and their ability to innovate."

1963: A YEAR TO REMEMBER

A well-known Ozarks woodcarver, Peter Engler, moved his shop to the City in 1963. Engler's meticulous craftsmanship drew crowds of people, who bought every piece he carved. The Herschends determined that other Ozarks crafts should be showcased. The first Missouri Festival of Ozark Craftsmen in 1963 featured native folks demonstrating woodcarving, tie hacking, shingle splitting, blacksmithing, weaving and lye soap and candle making.

That year, 500,000 people visited the park, and Silver Dollar City became Missouri's number one tourist attraction. The Herschends added resident craftsmen to the park: glassblower, weaver, potter and silversmith. The preservation of Ozarks crafts and the annual fall festival became hallmarks that turned into the National Festival of Craftsmen. Today, the annual event—named the National Harvest Festival—sets the stage under a canopy of autumn leaves for celebrations of the season, including crafts, music, food and special events.

HILLBILLIES MEET HILLBILLIES

Jack Herschend notes that the filming of six sequential episodes of *The Beverly Hillbillies*, the top-rated television show in the nation back in the 1960s, changed Silver Dollar City from a nice little park known from Buffalo, Missouri, to Harrison, Arkansas, into a phenomenon of mid-America.

"In 1969, our publicist, Don Richardson, proposed to *TV Guide* a story about a real hillbilly reviewing *The Beverly Hillbillies*," Jack says. "He found a young man, Junior Cobb, who had never seen the show. Don managed for Cobb to see the show, and his reactions turned into a story on the cover of the magazine."

"Don contacted Paul Henning, the show's creator, producer and director," Jack continues. "He suggested that Henning write several episodes in which the Hillbillies come home to Silver Dollar City. Henning loved the idea."

A cast and crew of fifty with five tons of equipment and props moved from Hollywood to Silver Dollar City, filming five episodes of the show with the premise of the Clampetts seeking a husband for Elly Mae (played by Donna Douglas). The *Hillbillies* cast turned Hannah's Ice Cream Parlor—one of the park's five original buildings—into their hotel. Shad Heller, the only professional performer from the City, fit right into the production. Because he was a quick study, Henning wrote the bearded smithy into a number of scenes. "Paul Henning gave a marvelous gift to Silver Dollar City," Jack states.

THE CITY EXPANDS INTO THE PAST

Mary Herschend's penchant for authenticity and preservation lives on in the themed rides, shows, festivals, characters, buildings and, particularly, the trees of the reproduction mountain village. Jack and Pete Herschend picked up where their parents left off, building Silver Dollar City on the mission statement: "Creating memories worth repeating." The 1800s theme park preserves the heritage of a past century in crafts and music yet utilizes the newest and most technologically advanced rides of the twenty-first century.

"When we add rides, shops, shows and theaters, we try to do it in a way that would be believable for the 1880s or early 1900s. We look at historic stories and themes—what could have been," states General Manager Brad Thomas.

Fulfilling the rumor that Marmaros had a saloon, the Silver Dollar Saloon opened in 1973 with cancan dancers and singing bartenders serving up root beer. Early on, Carrie Nation and her temperance union beat on the doors, demanding to close down the house. She never won. And from year to year, the show changed. Typically, Mean Murphy remains the saloon's arch enemy, and Miss Tilly charms the audience with ditzy innocence.

The glory days of mining continues to blast off in roller coasters, such as Fire in the Hole and PowderKeg, named the Best Family Thrill Coaster on the Planet by www.thrillride.com. Fashioned after the long-ago powder mills that turned the nitrogen-rich bat guano into black powder, PowderKeg moves its cars onto the launching pad amid rocking and tipping jars of nitroglycerine. The nitro "explodes," and the cars blast out of the building and over the City's birthright, Marvel Cave. Fire and smoke in special effects shoot through the roof of the powder mill load station.

Silver Dollar
City Saloon
proprietors.
*Courtesy of Silver
Dollar City Archives.*

Silver Dollar City's
PowderKeg roller
coaster. *Courtesy of
Arline Chandler.*

WildFire, the park's tallest and fastest coaster, takes its theme from the story of an old Ozarks inventor, Dr. Harris, who obsessed over creating a powered flying contraption for flight across the Ozarks. WildFire is the fuel that the doctor developed for his flying machine.

"We are not a Colonial Williamsburg, nor a living history museum," Thomas explains. "We are a park with a theme. We create the atmosphere of an 1880 mining town, paying tribute to the village that would have been here when the miners were in the cave. Everything we build looks to the past."

Thomas explains that the planning team wanted an old Ozarks barn swing. "We went out and found the ride, created the setting of a 1880s family farm, and built the barn around the ride," he says.

The Great Swing, Silver Dollar City. *Courtesy of Lee Smith.*

The Giant Swing bursts through the huge red barn, swinging riders at roller coaster speed more than seven stories into the treetops. A ten-foot copper rooster weathervane, made by one of the park's craftsmen, tops the barn's roof. The area includes other activities, such as cow milking and jumbo checkers games. Farm fruits, vegetables and hand-churned ice cream reflect the rural-life theme.

"Our approach was different for Tom and Huck's RiverBlast," Thomas says. "We found this fun ride that is interactive and suitable for all ages and sizes of people. We looked for story lines to theme the ride. Our good Missouri boys, Tom Sawyer and Huck Finn, fit. From the stories of Mark Twain, we re-created a setting for this ride."

When Silver Dollar City determined to build an exhibition hall that could accommodate large shows, dining or the city of Bethlehem at Christmas, they looked to the Red Gold of the Ozarks—tomato growing and canning. During the Great Depression, the rough, rocky Ozarks ground cleared of trees proved the perfect soil for growing the red jeweled fruit as a cash crop. Red Gold Heritage Hall resembles one of the numerous canning factories set up in Ozarks towns close to a steady supply of water.

Continuing to expand on historical themes, Silver Dollar City increased its rides by 50 percent in 2006, creating the Grand Exhibition area for families and children. Thomas says, "From visitor surveys, we discovered families wanted more rides they could enjoy together. Listening to our guests, we built kid-friendly rides from the high-flying swing to a family-sized coaster. Seven rides accommodate parents with their kids, and three rides permit smaller kids to ride alone."

In accordance to preserving the history and heritage of the Ozarks, the Silver Dollar City planning team chose a theme inspired by the world's fairs and expositions of more than one hundred years ago. "As the traveling expositions drew people from hundreds of miles around to marvel at the latest mechanical innovations and American ingenuity, Silver Dollar City's Grand Exposition complements our trademark—bringing the past to life," says Thomas. "We chose décor, details and colors from graphics and artwork showcased at the 1876 Philadelphia Exposition, the 1893 Chicago World's Fair and the 1904 St. Louis World's Fair. The rides aren't 1880s rides, but the ambiance of the area takes people back to another time."

COOKIN' UP OZARKS VITTLES

From cakes cooking on an old-fashioned hoe during the Annual Harvest Festival to summer snap beans simmering at the McHaffie Homestead, Silver Dollar City's mouthwatering food summons memories of hearth and home. Whiffs of old-time cooking drift over the City's treetops: succotash and calico potatoes simmering in a wagon wheel-sized skillet, chocolate fudge poured from a copper pot onto a marble slab at Brown's Candy Shop, kettle corn stirred in an oversized popper, corn in the shuck roasting alongside barbecue ribs, strawberries and cream, fried chicken and beans and ham bubbling in a black iron kettle. Restaurants and food carts dot the park, offering options for sit-down dining or a meal on the go.

In case folks want to learn how to turn an Ozarks recipe into a tempting dish, the Culinary & Craft School, housed in a turn-of-the century farm cottage, offers daily cooking classes. A

Hoecakes cooking on a garden hoe at Silver Dollar City. *Courtesy of Arline Chandler.*

Debbie Dance Uhrig, master craftswoman of culinary arts, presents classes at the Culinary & Craft School, Silver Dollar City. *Courtesy of Silver Dollar City.*

timber frame structure—its wraparound porch overlooking Echo Hollow—the school is a blend of American heritage and a state-of-the-art kitchen and classroom. Silver Dollar City craftsmen decorated and furnished the house with hand-carved front doors, a chip-carved wood mantle, hammered copper tiles framing the fireplace, handmade furniture and a six-foot chandelier with five hundred amber blown-glass spheres.

ONE TICKET, MULTIPLE SHOWS

Silver Dollar City opened in 1960, with the Mabe brothers making Ozarks music on homemade instruments. Since that day, music, comedy and playacting have been signatures of the city—resonating on stages and inside theaters that one by one cropped up as the village spread to more than fifty acres. Some are outdoor venues seating up to 150 and featuring regular entertainers, as well as guest groups. Echo Hollow, the park's outdoor amphitheater, seats 4,000 people. Others, such as Riverfront Playhouse and the 1,000-seat Opera House, are indoor venues, offering a variety of acts. Typically, the opera house hosts Broadway-type productions—*Headin' West,*

Flag thrower from Italy at
WorldFest, Silver Dollar City.
Courtesy of Arline Chandler.

a musical tale of American westward expansion during the 1860s, and *A Christmas Carol*, an adaption of Charles Dickens's Christmas classic.

At the McHaffie Homestead, Ozarks pickers sit on the front porch and entertain folks just as Ozarks families have done for generations—no frills, no amplification, just the strum of guitars and banjos and a clear melody from an old-time fiddle.

Throughout the operating season, Silver Dollar City hosts six different festivals. WorldFest, an international event showcasing different cultures and performers from around the world, kicks off in the spring. The Bluegrass & BBQ Festival celebrates stringed music and tasty ribs from across the nation. The National Kids' Fest fills the summer months, followed by Southern Gospel Picnic in late August. The National Harvest Festival features visiting craftsmen and American music. An Old Time Christmas rounds out the year with four million twinkling lights and a five-story special effects Christmas tree centering the town square.

SILVER DOLLAR CITY'S FUTURE IN THE OZARKS PAST

Despite the high-quality production entertainment and up-to-the-minute rides, Silver Dollar City stays true to its old-fashioned atmosphere. Folks still meander along tree-shaded walkways that curve, bend and climb hills. Kids are still deputized by the town marshal. Gospel songs float on a breeze from the century-old Wilderness Church. Visitors run their fingers over waxy bars of homemade lye soap or touch the soft featherbed in McHaffie Cabin. The blacksmith's hammer rings against an iron anvil, and his open-air forge blazes hot. Craftsmen throughout the park demonstrate their techniques and share their history. And always, faces smile and citizens say, "Howdy!"

Recognized worldwide, Silver Dollar City won the 1998–99 Applause Award, the theme park industry's top award of excellence based on management, operations, creativity and ingenuity. The park was also the 2001 recipient of the prestigious Thea Classic Award, recognizing worldwide excellence and outstanding achievement in themed entertainment from the Themed Entertainment Association.

In 2009, Silver Dollar City was named the Friendliest Park in the Golden Ticket Awards hosted by the *Amusement Today* newspaper. From international polls, *Amusement Today* defines "Best of the Best" in the amusement industry. The old-time city won second in Best Christmas Event, second in Best Food, third in Best Shows and fifth in Best Landscaping.

According to Pete Hershend:

> *The operational strategy of Silver Dollar City is anchored around special events. But the creative gems of the City lie in both little and big touches from our "citizens." Andy Miller's design for the look of the blacksmith shop's roof, windows slightly askew, the watering tree—the list goes on and on. If we ever walk away from touching people's lives in big and little ways, we will change the character of the company.*

CHAPTER 5

CITIZENS OF THE CITY

The buildings of Silver Dollar City are nothing without the "somebody" in them.
—Pete Herschend, cofounder, Silver Dollar City

Since Silver Dollar City opened on May 1, 1960, more than sixty-five million guests have stepped into the past century. Over the years, more than thirty-five thousand smiling "somebodies" have greeted folks in the shops, on the streets and near the rides in the City—or at other venues in the Branson area owned by Herschend Family Entertainment, Inc.

General Manager Brad Thomas relates an early story about a building that cofounder Jack Herschend planned to locate next to the exit of the cable train. "Russ Pearson showed up and told Jack to do nothing until he returned with a model of the town square. Jack listened—and waited.

"Then Andy Miller envisioned the park almost as a movie set," Thomas continues. "Those early decisions created the charm and atmosphere we have today."

He goes on to say that Andy Miller, Russ Pearson, Don Richardson and Shad Heller, Silver Dollar City's blacksmith and first mayor, plus hundreds of others brought the right skills to lead the Herschend family through a particular era. "Yet the Herschends created an environment in which people wanted to give their ideas," Thomas says. "Not only did the Herschends listen, but the opinions and ideas of others formulated much of what we have today."

The company now calls its relationship with employees "servant leadership," meaning that the leaders of the company listen to the visitors as well as to the "citizens" who work at Silver Dollar City.

SHAD HELLER EMBODIED THE SPIRIT OF THE OZARKS

Pete Herschend sums up the spirit of Silver Dollar City in the memory of Shad Heller. A man totally in step with the nineteenth century, Shad Heller immersed himself in the peculiar mix of myth and reality in the Ozarks. Moving to Branson with his wife, Ruth, in the late 1950s, the former vaudevillian and circus clown landed the part of the Old Shepherd in an early stage adaptation of *The Shepherd of the Hills* at Beacon Hill Theatre. Ruth played Aunt Mollie.

In 1960, Heller helped develop the *Shepherd of the Hills* outdoor drama, which opened at the Shepherd of the Hills Homestead the same summer that Silver Dollar City unlocked its shops and attractions. Both Shad and Ruth were hired at the new theme park to create characters and "atmosphere shows" for daytime entertainment. Drawing from his humor, keen wit and strong character, Shad combined early Ozarks blacksmithing with his gift for drama. At the Wilderness Road Blacksmith Shop, Aunt Mollie (as Ruth was known) sold the wares he hammered and fired in his forge. Over the years, Heller became the "official" mayor of Silver Dollar City, population twenty-eight.

Jack Herschend recalls: "Shad's eyes danced as soon as he stepped into a role." One day, Heller played the sheriff. Another, he feuded with the Hatfields against the McCoys. The spontaneous and unscripted shows—played to the hilt on a dirt street—often drew unsuspecting visitors into scenes with schoolmarms, gaudy saloon girls, city slickers, medicine show professors and sometimes gullible hill folks. In most of the hillbilly nonsense, Heller turned the jokes on the characters themselves. Both Mollie and Shad Heller created characters and stunts to entertain guests on the City's streets.

Shad Heller, Silver Dollar City's blacksmith and first mayor. *Courtesy of Silver Dollar City Archives.*

Many local entertainers credit their early training and experience to the Hellers. The couple recognized a common love of theater and vaudeville in Terry Bloodworth, one of Silver Dollar City's master glass blowers. Heller approached Bloodworth with the idea of writing a new version of an old vaudeville act, *The Toby Show.*

During the 1970s, the Hellers, with Bloodworth's input, produced and starred in their own *Corn Crib Theatre Toby Show*—one of the initial presentations on 76 Music Country Boulevard in Branson. For sixteen years, the popular show entertained thousands of visitors and trained dozens of actors.

Early on, Don Richardson, Silver Dollar City's publicist, launched a promotional tour, carrying Ozarks craftspeople to the world via television and radio. From Detroit to Houston—and occasionally to Hollywood—Richardson and Pete Herschend handled the logistics, while the craftsmen demonstrated their crafts on the road. Shad Heller fabricated a traveling forge to show off blacksmithing. Once, he played the musical saw on *What's My Line?* Well-known television personality Arlene Francis guessed his identity. After *The Beverly Hillbillies* left Silver Dollar City, Shad Heller flew to Los Angeles and filmed at least fifteen more episodes with the cast.

Today, every ring of the blacksmith's hammer—and every hillbilly prank that creates a memory—celebrates the man who embodied the sum and substance of Silver Dollar City.

KEEP THE SHOW ALIVE AND GOING

Over the past three decades, actor Terry Sanders, once mentored by Shad Heller, remembers the old actor's counsel: "Don't let Corn Crib die," referring to his vaudeville-type entertainment at the Branson theater where Sanders thought he had his first "big break."

"The Hellers actually put me to work parking cars and selling concessions," Sanders says. "From the sidelines, I watched and memorized all the lines of the act. One night, Ruth Heller paged me to fill a role. For the next three years, I played different characters in *The Toby Show.*"

At Silver Dollar City, Sanders first played Mr. M. Balmer. His job? Measuring guests. "I do the character in mime, and I hear all sorts of comments because people think I'm mechanical," he says. "But I've been known to step out of character and chase a guest across the park!"

One day at the City's Tintype Shop, other characters brainstormed to dress Sanders as Granny McCoy. "While goofing off in the Ice Cream Parlor, I drew a small crowd. In my high-pitched Granny voice, I said the Hatfields were outside," he remembers. "With my gun, I tapped the window pane—

and it shattered. Not really part of my act!"

For gigs at the Braschlers' Theater in Branson, Sanders polished his impersonations of Joan Rivers and Barney Fife, as well as janitor Homer Lee. In 1990 and 1991, he appeared as a guest on several segments of national television's *Hee Haw*. However, he returned to the Ozarks. The heart of a true comic beats under a Joan Rivers dress; the fine suit of Atlanta's banker, Colonel Paisley Alowishous Parnell; or the frazzled lab coat of Silver Dollar City's WildFire inventor. Armed with a degree in theater from Missouri State University, Sanders built his career on characters on the

Actor Terry Sanders as janitor Homer Lee.
Courtesy of Terry Sanders.

city's streets, the dirt-floored stage of *The Shepherd of the Hills* and the spotlight of Branson's theaters.

CHARACTERS IN THE OZARKS CULTURE

"Silver Dollar City's culture is a natural part of the Ozarks," says Brad Thomas. "Although many Silver Dollar City employees have come from 'off,' as hill folks say, they fit into the culture—the mindset that we're going to work hard but have fun. Bonnie Borden is an example."

With two kids, four dogs and twelve horses, Borden moved from southern California to the Missouri Ozarks "to raise my kids at a slower pace with clean air and midwestern values," she says.

She discovered Silver Dollar City, and the City discovered her background in theater. "I put everything into the characters I portrayed in street scenes and guest interactions," Borden says. "I soaked up the histories of the hearty mountain folks—those who struggled in the Ozarks to eke out a living."

Borden played the first Carrie Nation, beating down the door of the saloon. She moved to the City's streets and played both Ma McCoy and Ma Hatfield in different seasons. "I acted the roles of everybody, from a crusty old mining woman to a rainmaker. I put the stories I learned into my characters, not to poke fun but to *have* fun in a zany kind of way. I have an admiration for the people who didn't follow the wagon trains west looking for something better. They stayed here and worked hard in the harsh hills."

She also made a concerted effort to master the Ozarks dialect. "I was out on the street one day, performing one of our ridiculous skits. A lady came up to me and said, 'Honey, I flew all the way from California to see a genuine hillbilly, and you are

A transplanted hillbilly, Bonnie Borden. *Courtesy of Silver Dollar City.*

it!' To me, that proved that guests who come to Silver Dollar City want to believe—if only for a few moments," she says with a laugh.

Before his retirement, Roscoe Moore, a Wisconsin postal worker, and his wife visited Silver Dollar City. When he walked through the door of the 1890s-styled bakery, he pointed to the baker and said, "That's the job I'm going to have when I retire." And he did.

"When guests came into the bakery, I watched them inhale and say 'ahhh,'" he says. "The smell of baking bread brings back memories of grandma's house, and I loved being a part of that memory."

A Badge on His Vest, a Bible Next to His Heart

Bob Deeds retired as pastor of a United Methodist Church in northern Missouri but wanted to be productive. He took his résumé to Silver Dollar City, and they hired him to work in the gun shop. "I thought I'd do that for a season and then start some kind of ministry," he says.

However, Deeds found his ministry as the City's marshal and part-time circuit-riding preacher. Former members of his congregations were a bit taken aback when they visited Silver Dollar City and saw their dignified silver-haired minister toting a six-shooter and racing around the streets acting out silly episodes with other characters.

On Sundays, he switched roles and costumes to become a real-life pastor to the park's Wilderness Church, holding early morning worship services for park employees and guests. He officiated at weddings and marriage vow renewals. Behind his shiny marshal's badge, Deeds had a listening heart for guests who sought his counsel.

HANDMADE KNIVES AND HOMESPUN POETRY

While Borden, Deeds and Moore retired after a couple of decades in their newfound roles, knife maker Ray Johnson continues to pull his blades from a blazing forge and pound them into shape against his anvil. As he hammers and thrusts the sharpened steel into a metal barrel to test its strength, he recites his own philosophy on life—often in rhyme.

"I've built hundreds of knives from every kind of metal, including truck springs and old saw blades," he says. "Sometimes, your grandfather's ways were the hardest and slowest, but the best."

"I've taken the best of old ways and combined them with the best in modern metallurgy to create my knives," he continues. "I'm just egotistical enough to believe that when this earth is finished, there will be a few pieces of rusty old blades lying around with 'Ray Johnson' engraved on them."

Knife maker and poet Ray Johnson demonstrates his skill at Silver Dollar City. *Courtesy of Lee Smith.*

McHaffie Cabin: A Working Homestead

At theaters across Silver Dollar City, performers such as Cedric Benoit and his Cajun Connection entertain with polished musical skills. But McHaffie Homestead offers a peek into genuine hillbilly life as it happened more than a century back. The folks who hang out every day at the homestead smoke their own meats, gather eggs and pull radishes from the garden. Dinner is served at noon—an old-time meal cooked in the cabin's kitchen on a wood stove. Everybody has a name—Cousin Clem, Aunt Fannie, Uncle Jeb. The ladies of the homestead bake cornbread and cook greens and beans seasoned with salt pork. Visiting children cuddle a baby chick and hang over a railing of the pen to watch piglets. After chores, the men gather on the front porch to entertain guests sitting here and there on a stone wall, a tree stump or in a cane-bottom chair. A few wander through the old Ozarks living quarters. Strains of century-old ballads or gospel songs lift to the treetops and mingle with smells of home cooking.

Wandering Minstrel of the Ozarks

Danny Eakin, dubbed a wandering minstrel, started his romance with Silver Dollar City as an eager-eyed eight-year-old on his first visit to the reproduction mining town. "I remember the taste of funnel cakes and the late Shad Heller's welcoming face under his brushy, gray beard," Eakin recalls, closing his eyes to recall the smells of burning coals in the old blacksmith shop. "I remember Jim Bass hewing logs and the old barn that reminded me of my grandpa. He taught me to plow, sing gospel songs and just plain relax. I thought: This is some kind of place!"

An Ozarks minstrel, Danny Eakin, and one of his blue tick pups. *Courtesy of Arline Chandler.*

Eakin says that stories, humor and music run in his family. He grew up in Arkansas plowing with mules and listening to the baying of coon dogs. As a boy, Eakin's bedroom faced seventy-eight acres of wilderness bound by a hollow that led to a creek—making a perfect place for dogs to run.

"When hunters let their dogs go every Saturday night, they ran up that 'holler,' and I started mocking their howls," he says. "By midnight, I had every dog in the county barking under my bedroom window. They thought I had a coon up a tree! Now, I'm best known for imitating an old blue tick hound. Here at the City, I might be strumming my guitar and singing a love song. If someone yells out, 'Where's Old Blue?' I just throw in a yelp right there in the middle of that verse."

BACKING UP EACH OTHER'S STORIES

Richard Young and his wife Judy—Aunt Judy to guests at McHaffie Homestead—both come from storytelling families. Judy expected to teach

Storyteller Judy Young at McHaffie Homestead, Silver Dollar City. *Courtesy of Silver Dollar City.*

children. After a couple of terms as a high school teacher, she worked her first season at Silver Dollar City making lye soap and robbing trains. Once she started "entertaining the masses," as she describes her role at the city, she made no plans to resume teaching. With dramatic and mind-boggling tales, punctuated with sweeping arm gestures and eyebrows arched over expressive eyes—she engages folks.

"I started a silly audience-involved street show called "The Schoolmarm and the Bear,'" she says. "In the fall, when kids returned to school, I began telling stories to have something to do when tour buses carried older folks to the city."

At that point, she actively sought and collected stories. "People from everywhere tell me wonderful tales and family history," she says.

Two seasons after Judy began her oral story collection, Richard Young took summers from his teaching job to become a character actor at Silver Dollar City. The two, drawn together by a common interest in preserving tales of the past, partnered in both professions and marriage. Richard, now retired from education, works across the park—his job described as "crowd controller."

"I atmosphere an area," he says, "meaning I visit with folks while they wait in line for Riverfront Playhouse and, later, I announce the show." He notes that guests try to trick him into stepping out of character, asking, "What year is this? Who is president?"

I answer, "Why, it's 1892, and Grover Cleveland is our president!'"

Back at McHaffie Homestead, Aunt Judy invites folks to step inside her home. "She often tells outlaw stories. Traditionally, an Ozarks woman would not have told such tales around the fireplace," Richard says. "We're stretching rules a bit with Judy telling stories that didn't actually happen in the imaginary family living in the cabin."

However, some of the stories she tells are documented facts about the cabin and three generations of McHaffies who called it home when it sat on the banks of Swan Creek near Forsythe, Missouri. With a voice that resonates like a dinner bell, she invites folks in and immediately picks up on their comments that the cabin is *big* compared to others of the area.

"Course, when yore a-startin' a cabin, you only have to have four things—good stout walls, a roof that don't leak, a door that nothing can get in through and a fireplace," she explains in Ozarks vernacular. "Everything else is optional. Floors? Just put up with what you got—even if it's dirt. And winders? Just open the door to let in some light. If the sun's down, you oughta be in bed anyhow!"

Aunt Judy's favorite guests come in small sizes. Once a young boy pointed to the old porcelain chamber pot sitting on the rafters of what had been the cabin's sleeping loft. He asked, "What's that white thing?"

"I explained about the 'slop jar,' but it took a while! When he finally understood, he was outraged," she says. "'Why didn't they just flush the toilet?' he asked."

BEHIND THE SCENES OR SERVING UP FRONT

Over the years, Silver Dollar City has hired—and continues to hire—numerous retired and second-career people from all walks of life. Many play roles such as the marshal, the baker, the candlestick maker—all characters from a century ago. Many others work behind the scenes to keep the city humming—carpenters, costume seamstresses, cooks and servers in restaurants and clerks in shops. The various citizens get caught up in the spirit of the past and bring a multitude of talents to all divisions of the park. Some are "image makers," greeting tour buses and giving directions around the winding walkways. All employees working in visible roles dress in typical 1890s garb—some obviously more affluent than others. The long calico skirt and bonnet of a woman serving bottled sodas, roasted nuts or home-baked cookies contrasts with the summertime guests in shorts, sandals and T-shirts.

Pete Herschend notes: "Although many workers are from other places, they pick up this culture, handed down in oral tradition. One says to another, 'This is how we take care of people's needs.' You can't script that. You have to have an environment that encourages that kind of interaction."

Jack Herschend picks up Pete's words. "Empowerment is a big part of our company's relationship with employees, but it's more that we care for one another," he says as a springboard to one of his favorite stories about Silver Dollar City's citizens, which follows.

A STREET SWEEPER WITH A POCKETFUL OF SILVER DOLLARS

"Luke Standlee worked for over thirty years pouring hot asphalt," Jack continues. "He thought he'd died and gone to heaven when he got a retirement job sweeping our streets. Slim as a pine sapling—standing over six feet tall—he loved to lay aside his broom and clog to the music of the Horse Creek Band."

One day, Jack wandered through the park and happened to see Standlee on his knees, talking to a little girl, her parents standing aside. When the family walked away all smiles and he straightened to stand, Jack asked what had happened.

Shuffling his feet in his work shoes, Standlee said, "Shucks, it was nothing. Whenever I see little kids who are disabled or having a hard time, I talk to them and hand them a silver dollar."

Jack says, "We had no idea that Luke Standlee was using his own money to enrich a child's life. But that's an example of the empowerment our citizens act upon—seeing a need and fulfilling it on the spot. From that day on, the company filled Luke Standlee's pockets with silver dollars."

Luke Standlee clogging with Horse Creek Band at Silver Dollar City. *Courtesy of Arline Chandler.*

June Ward Leads the Sweetest Shop in Town

Master candy maker June Ward is on a first-name basis with Santa—and with the owners of Silver Dollar City, Jack and Pete Herschend. She comes from Stone County, Missouri, and grew up in Ozarks culture. Her homespun philosophy fits her claim that the city's executive office is actually in the Brown Candy Shop's kitchen.

Brad Thomas agrees, remembering numerous mornings when he, Jack Herschend and other heads of departments sampled candy and discussed park matters around the table in the corner. "June operated the board room and impacted many of our lives with her personality, humor and hard work ethic," he says.

Thomas laughs about employee photographs Ward hangs in the candy shop, tagged as "Silver Dollar City Employee of the Year." A few years ago, a lead in another area looked at those photographs and questioned June about why the workers in her shop received the awards.

Thomas continues, "June hugged her and replied, 'Darlin' the cream always rises to the top!' The other employee left and life went on. What

Master candy maker June Ward in Brown's Candy Kitchen at Silver Dollar City. *Courtesy of Silver Dollar City.*

June did not explain is the fact that Silver Dollar City has no 'Employee of the Year.' Whenever June determines, she sends her workers to the Tintype Shop to be photographed. Then she has a little engraved plaque made and hangs it on the wall. This typifies our employees' mindset—working hard, but having fun with the job."

Thomas sums up his admiration for the city's employees in his acceptance of the Friendliest Park award at LEGOLAND in Carlsbad, California. He said, "For more than five decades, Silver Dollar City has been about our people. They create the heart and soul of the park. The friendliness of our staff defines this company."

CHAPTER 6

A BAND OF BROTHERS CALLED BALDKNOBBERS

Our show has always been about our family entertaining your family.
—Tim Mabe, Baldknobbers' producer and comedian

A half century ago, Ozarks folks created their own entertainment with play parties, fox hunts, cakewalks and pie suppers. "All around the Ozarks, men got together, turned their dogs loose, built up a bonfire and sat around socializing and listening to their hounds howl as they chased a fox," says Brent Mabe, son of Lyle and Betty Mabe, one of the four Mabe couples who cofounded the Baldknobbers Jamboree Show. "Those men decided they wanted some entertainment before they ran the dogs, so my dad and his brothers went out to pick and sing for them and tell some jokes."

By 1959—long before the words "live music show capital" were whispered—the Mabe brothers (Jim, Bill, Lyle and Bob) had become so popular with the locals that they decided fishermen on Lake Taneycomo might pay for entertainment in the evenings. They dressed in overalls and hillbilly hats and played music on the second floor of Branson's old city hall, furnished with fifty folding chairs. Their wives, clad in long calico dresses, sold tickets and concessions. Before the show, they paraded Branson's streets with handmade placards reading "Country Music—This Way!" If twelve guests bought tickets, they performed. If not, Jim Mabe asked folks to return the next evening to make up a larger crowd.

"Our dads were on stage, so our moms sewed costumes, ushered, took tickets, sold souvenirs and concessions and did what they called 'check

Baldknobbers cofounders, *left to right*, include Bill Mabe, Jim Mabe as Droopy Drawers Jr. and Lyle Mabe as George Aggernite. In the center is the family's matriarch, Hazel Mabe. *Courtesy of Baldknobbers Archives.*

out,' which meant they counted the money," says second-generation Baldknobber Tim Mabe, son of Jim and Katie Mabe. "They were an integral part of the show."

"My dad and uncles chose downtown because in the late 1950s, the action happened there. The 'strip' was a lonely two-lane Highway 76 leading outside town to Marvel Cave several miles away," Tim continues. "Table Rock Dam had just been completed, so downtown Branson had the biggest concentration of resorts, guests and visitors—folks who mainly came to fish."

Taking the name "Baldknobbers" from an Ozarks secretive vigilante group that met on the mountains' bald knobs in the late 1800s, the Mabes belted out harmonies they had developed from years of singing in church—the sons of the humble Reverend Donald Mabe. They backed up their country, bluegrass and gospel music with homemade instruments. A washtub bass, flat-top guitars, an old washboard for rhythm and the jawbone of a mule substituting for drums were typical in homes around the Ozarks.

"In 1960, my dad and uncles performed on opening day at Silver Dollar City, and they were in the original cast of the *Shepherd of the Hills* outdoor drama," says Brent. "We all believe 1960 was a pivotal year. Without the opening of Silver Dollar City and *Shepherd of the Hills*, Branson would not be what it is today."

WHY BALDKNOBBERS?

"Most of us from the Ozarks know about Bald Knobbers," Tim Mabe says, explaining that the original group of men organized in 1885 in Taney County, under the direction of a Civil War veteran named Nat Kinney. He gathered upstanding men from the county to become a Law and Order League. They committed to a secret oath and learned a secret grip and a password. Their mission was to restore law and order to Taney County.

Other groups were formed in Christian and Douglas Counties—starting with the same values as the Law and Order League. Those groups abruptly turned to harassment of farmers, lumbermen and merchants, as well as their families. They rode at night using signal fires set on bald knobs of the hills to call their groups together. These men wore black hooded masks with red embroidery outlining eye and mouth holes, topped with long tassels that resembled horns.

Kinney officially disbanded the Taney County Bald Knobbers on April 8, 1886, but the lawless groups from other counties continued to terrorize Ozarks folks until the hangings of leaders on May 10, 1889. Harold Bell Wright kept the legend of the Bald Knobbers alive in his novel *Shepherd of the Hills*.

"Dad said that everyone who came to the area wanted to see a hillbilly, and with the rich history of the area, it just made sense to call themselves one word—the Baldknobbers," Tim continues.

THE BALDKNOBBERS' BEGINNING

The Baldknobbers Jamboree became an immediate hit with fishermen and tourists to the Branson lakes area. "Grandpa used to say if the fishermen brought their wives to the show, they got to stay and fish another day," says Joy Bilyeu, granddaughter of Bill Mabe and a third-generation vocalist in today's show.

Brent Mabe, who currently leads the band, remembers when he and Tim earned fifty cents each putting bumper stickers advertising the Baldknobbers on cars. "For a free Coke, we did some cleanup in the old makeshift theater," he says. "At the shows today, fans remember my cousins and me playing ball in the parking lot with a crushed-up soda cup while our dads performed onstage."

To make ends meet financially, the brothers worked second jobs as gunfighters on Silver Dollar City's Main Street. In odd hours, they drove

A line of fans at the Baldknobbers' theater on Branson's Highway 76. *Courtesy of Baldknobbers Archives.*

around in a van topped with a PA system blaring information to attract visitors to their evening shows. During winter months, when entertainment closed in Branson, they braved icy roads and drafty auditoriums to perform road shows and draw tourists to their Ozark hometown for the summer season. Those early entrepreneurs had no idea that their show would start a tradition that would later become the "Live Music Show Capital of the World."

Once the family band outgrew city hall, they moved to the Sammy Lane Pavilion. By 1963, more than a dozen people showed up every night, and the Baldknobbers moved into a renovated skating rink.

"The show was regularly scheduled in the evenings throughout the summer and early fall," Brent Mabe says. "It was a real theater, with a stage and theater seats. Stage lights were sometimes on—and sometimes off. Not the production value we have today, but it was a real live music theater."

In 1968, the Mabes moved to their present location on Highway 76, across the road from where the Presley family had started performing the previous year. Brent Mabe still remembers, "Moving to the strip was a major decision. Dad and my uncles were scared to death because they quit day jobs and put everything into a music show business."

ONE EXTENDED FAMILY ENTERTAINING OTHER FAMILIES

The production started as a family affair and today continues with second- and third-generation Mabes—six on stage and nine working out front, Brent Mabe says. "I slept in a guitar case backstage when I was a baby. I've been in music all my life. We're planning to see fourth-, fifth- and, *probably*, sixth-generation Mabes in future shows."

"My son is fourteen, and he's not quite the hillbilly that I am," Brent continues. "But he's likely the one kid in Nixa High School who knows all the words to 'Your Mother's Not Dead, She's Only Sleeping,' an old hillbilly bluegrass song."

From the beginning, country music and hillbilly comedy defined the Baldknobbers. Their homespun humor gave the band of brothers a trademark outside of Branson. Lyle Mabe's comic character "George Aggernite" acted on television commercials for Empire Gas, which aired during the weather portion of the evening newscast at a Springfield television station. His rubbery face and mispronunciations flashed across television screens in countless homes from Springfield to Joplin and all over the Ozarks. The commercials also featured takeoffs of television shows and other product promotions. The face of a Baldknobber visited living rooms of Ozarks families every evening. Folks became fans—and friends—before ever seeing the stage show in Branson.

Through the years, the theater has had four renovations and now seats 1,700 people. The Baldknobbers' nineteen-member cast still entertains audiences with solid country, bluegrass, gospel and a distinctive brand of hillbilly humor.

A CHARACTER IS CREATED

The late Jim Mabe, originator of the character of Droopy Drawers, admitted he had a split personality—joking that some folks called it "cracked." Jim related in a 1999 interview for *Active Years* that he and his brothers grew up singing as a quartet on radio and for weddings and funerals. "When we started our show, I'd never done comedy," he said. "But I put on some droopy pants and a slouch hat and started pantomiming behind my brothers when they sang. I built my character as a quiet, insecure guy."

He described himself as very opposite offstage, sociable with people and enthusiastic in running the business the Baldknobbers expanded to include a restaurant and motel. "But once I put that costume on and got onstage in front of an audience, I automatically became Droopy Drawers."

Upon his father's retirement in 1997, Tim Mabe became Droopy Drawers Jr. "My dad and uncles founded the hillbilly humor of the Baldknobbers on the adage of the city slicker who comes to town to take advantage of the old hillbilly. However, the hillbilly gets the last laugh. The jokes are different today, but over fifty years later, that theme holds true."

Baldknobbers publicist Hollye Gurley says, "When Tim decided to try comedy on his own, he imagined the son of Droopy Drawers," she says, "childish and innocent like his dad's character, yet different. He added the bucked teeth to make his character's appearance different. Jim Mabe as Droopy Drawers never talked, but Tim chimes in now and again, primarily repeating what one of the other comedians says—indicating he has no original thoughts."

"Stepping into Dad's shoes was a big leap for me," Tim says. He believes that truly being the son of Droopy Drawers paved the way for audiences to accept his character.

"Droopy Drawers Jr. basically mimics what my dad created—the out-of-step hillbilly who is always in the wrong place onstage," he continues. "I work in tandem with comedian Stub Meadows to create scenes and pull jokes on the musicians and vocalists…as they try to keep their performances serious."

STUB MEADOWS: A TRUE HILLBILLY

Stub Meadows is always Stub—a nickname his uncle gave him as a boy. For close to three decades, the down-home comedian at the Baldknobbers Jamboree Show is the same Stub Meadows who lives on a farm that was homesteaded by his great-grandmother in the late 1880s. He's the same laidback Stub who flashes an innocent but startled look when his straight man, Bob Leftridge, confronts him with obvious information.

Baldknobbers' hillbillies, *left to right*: Hargus Marcel, Droopy Drawers Jr. and Stub Meadows. *Courtesy Baldknobbers Theater.*

Humor and storytelling come naturally to this native Missourian. "I can hear a line and build a story around it," he says, proving his point with the yarns he spins about coming from Burnt Mattress, Arkansas, which is right above Hot Springs.

On the stage that he shares with Droopy Drawers Jr., comedian Hargus Marcell and sixteen other cast members, Stub dresses up his overalls with a fancy shirt and a wide tie hanging to his knees. On occasion, he wears his baggy seersucker suit, telling the audience that Sears made it and he's the sucker who bought it.

Stub Meadows's timing for storytelling matches his rubber-faced expressions. He is adamant that he never practices his looks of shock, humor, disgust or innocence. Setting aside his teeth before going onstage, Stub easily pulls his lower lip over the upper lip, juts out his jaw and widens his eyes for an oblivious expression—now his trademark.

Hargus Marcel: Another Genuine Hillbilly

Jerl Adams has been tickling the funny bones of folks in the Ozarks for more than thirty-three years. Performing as his alter ego "Hargus Marcel," Jerl's interpretation of funny comes naturally. Taking "Marcel" from the late Jerry Clower's frequent reference to his friend, Marcel Ledbetter, Hargus Marcel rolls like Ozark molasses off Jerl's tongue. For twenty-two years, he portrayed the clueless country bumpkin at Pine Mountain Jamboree in Eureka Springs, Arkansas. After his move to Branson, he performed with Moe Bandy, *Country Tonite* and the Sons of the Pioneers at Shepherd of the Hills Homestead. He joined the comedy team at the Baldknobbers Jamboree in 2006.

The Cast

Over the years the cast has changed, adding Tim's wife, Patty, who comes from a musical family with Missouri roots. In 2006, their son, Brandon, brought the third generation of Mabes onto the stage. Brandon and Patty are both vocalists. Patty says, "We absolutely love what we do and are blessed to continue this unique style of family entertainment the Mabe brothers created in 1959."

Although the cast had impressive additions in 2006, they also suffered loss in the death of Dennis Mabe, son of founding member Bill Mabe. His sons,

Current performing Mabes, *left to right,* include Denton Mabe, Joy Bilyeu, Brent Mabe, Brandon Mabe, Patty Mabe and Tim "Droopy Drawers Jr." Mabe. *Courtesy of Baldknobbers Theater.*

Denton and Garrett, joined other third-generation cast members the same year that their cousin Brandon came onto the stage.

"Being on the show has been my goal since I was a little boy," Denton says. "I've looked up to my father and mentor, Dennis Mabe, all my life. I owe all of my drive and talent to him."

Joy Bilyeu, granddaughter of Baldknobbers cofounders Bill and Joyce Mabe, began her career as a vocalist at age three when her parents, Pastor Hosea and Debbie Bilyeu, started her singing for church congregations. After starring in a number of musical productions during her college days, Joy led the Baldknobbers cast as featured female vocalist for ten years before taking a sabbatical in 1999 to focus on raising her family and fulfilling missionary work in Peru, Guatemala and Mexico. She returned to the Baldknobbers stage in 2006.

In addition to family members who pick and sing, the Baldknobbers round out their cast with solid Ozarks entertainers like Bob Leftridge. As emcee, vocalist, guitarist and straight man for the antics of Stub Meadows and Hargus Marcel, Leftridge displays fresh reactions night after night to the outlandish stories the comedians concoct.

"Our comedians have a script," Brent Mabe says, "but we never know where a tall tale will take them. They weave into their acts a common thread of human experiences. Their perfectly timed routines are pure Americana."

"Everyone on stage plays at least a couple of instruments, and most all of us sing—even the comedians," he continues. "Many of the talented musicians and singers have been with our family for numerous years."

For several decades, Mike Ito—hailing from Tokyo, Japan—has performed with the Mabe family. He plays fiddle, mandolin and banjo and sings solo and harmony.

Other cast members, too numerous to name, have contributed to the success of the Baldknobbers. Brent Mabe recalls Max Tate, Howard Hale, Roger Blevins and Gene Dove, to name a few. Gene Dove says, "Seeing the younger generation of Baldknobbers take the reins of the show gives the old George Jones song, 'Who's Gonna Fill Their Shoes' a whole new meaning. The Baldknobbers Jamboree Show is in capable hands."

Tim explains, "The Baldknobbers show is entirely a group effort. Every cast member puts their stamp on new comedy, music and costumes each year. The show is our star. Dad taught me that!"

The beaded, glitzy outfits of today's singers and musicians contrast the hillbilly get-ups in the Baldknobbers' first shows. The fast-paced production with the latest lighting and sound sweeps its audience into a seamless evening of top-notch musical entertainment.

"From the very first show, the Baldknobbers sang gospel music," Tim adds. "Grandfather Mabe was a Baptist minister who instilled in all eleven of his children, and sixty-something of us grandkids, a love for Christ and the importance of family and faith to our everyday lives. That has not changed in over fifty years. Someone once said to my dad, 'I don't like country music, but I like the Baldknobbers.' Dad found that amusing because if it's not country, it doesn't go in the show."

"The Baldknobbers are known for great traditional country music, but we also add a lot of today's number one hits. Our variety appeals to all ages!" Brent Mabe interjects. "Yet, often when we add new songs to our show, fans request the ones we've been doing for years, and we pull them back into the format."

Tim Mabe notes: "Those four Mabe brothers started something special in 1959. I'm proud to carry on the family tradition of country music and comedy."

CHAPTER 7

THE PRESLEYS

A Family Affair

The greatest compliment our fans have ever given is their loyalty, letting our family entertain their families with our own brand of music, humor and faith.

—*The Presleys*

Gary Presley, oldest son and president of Presleys' Incorporated, remembers cracking the door of their first theater on the curvy, two-lane Highway 76 to count the intermittent headlights filing past. He prayed they would turn in.

A few did. And for two hours, his family entertained other families with foot-stomping music and clean comedy. Then Gary recalls sweeping up the popcorn and the theater's only profit: a few coins dropped with the trash.

The Presleys trace their Ozarks roots back to 1850, but their current status as one of Branson's founding families of entertainment goes back to a hound dog and a guitar. Lloyd Presley, the family patriarch, courted the late Bessie Mae with a guitar in the backseat of his car—the same guitar his older brother, Don, had swapped a favorite hound dog to acquire. He carried that guitar on every date, but within his heart, he also carried a dream to earn his living playing music—a dream of his own theater with an actual stage, lights and sound.

In 1942, Lloyd married Bessie Mae Garrison. His produce delivery service to grocery stores in Springfield earned his family's living. The two dollars he made playing music on a flatbed truck on Saturday nights bought a few more groceries. But more significantly, performing at rural Missouri gatherings fed Lloyd's dream.

PAYING DUES

While the Presley family grew to include daughters Deanna and Janice and sons Gary and Steve, Lloyd teamed with the Luttrell brothers, Windy, Jim and Bill, to become the Ozark Playboys. The group performed all over southwest Missouri for local schools, corporation picnics or even grand openings of stores. Before long, the bluegrass band had a local thirty-minute weekly radio show on KGBX in Springfield. More importantly, the show, called *Saturday Night Jamboree*, preceded the national broadcast of the *Grand Ole Opry*. The Ozark Playboys developed a fan base, and Lloyd and Windy Luttrell formed an entertainment team that continued for five decades.

During the 1940s and early 1950s, Springfield nurtured a strategy for the Missouri city to challenge Nashville, Tennessee, as America's country music capital. An American network television show, *Ozark Jubilee*, originated from the heart of the Ozarks: Springfield, Missouri. The *Jubilee*—drawing more than nine million viewers and an equal number of listeners on ABC radio—launched or advanced the careers of several recording artists: Brenda Lee, June Carter Cash, Sonny James, Porter Wagoner, Chet Atkins and Jean Shephard, to name a few. Red Foley, at that time the nation's top country music star, hosted the show, which ended in 1960. Most of those bright young artists retreated to the *Grand Ole Opry* in Nashville. Who knew in the 1990s that Branson, not Springfield, would become Nashville's rival?

Although Lloyd Presley and the Ozark Playboys occasionally shared a stage with well-known country stars such as Buck Owens, they steadily continued to build solid fans. The homegrown musicians teamed with Loyd Evans, a deejay at KGBX, to perform in *The Country Caravan*, a long-running radio program that traveled and played one-night stands across Missouri. Evans booked them in a regular Saturday night show, *Farmarama*, at Springfield's Fantastic Caverns. By that time, eighteen-year-old Deanna and ten-year-old Janice joined the group as vocalists. Fourteen-year-old Gary played guitar. The radio station KGBX recorded and rebroadcast the show. A year later, Gary acted on Evans's suggestion to add comedy to the program. He borrowed a pair of size-fifty overalls from the closet of one grandpa and a pair of eyeglasses from the bureau of another.

"I found an old broken-down straw hat and blacked out my front teeth with an eyebrow pencil and walked onstage, not saying a word," he recalls. The audience laughed at his stereotypical hillbilly character, and Gary was hooked. He named himself "Herkimer," added one-liners and corny jokes and became the trademark for the Presleys' family show.

Their pace picked up when Lloyd, Gary and Janice also performed Monday through Friday nights in a cave close to Branson known as Underground Theatre. That show, called *The Tri-Lakes Opry*, was also recorded, rebroadcast and syndicated over the Midwest. The Presleys were paying dues and making a name.

During the day, Lloyd still ran his produce route. Bessie Mae worked full time at a typewriter factory in Springfield. And Lloyd, dressed as the "Friendly Fisherman," indulged his second passion—fishing—with a weekly report on KYTV (now KY-3) out of Springfield. In 1965, nine-year-old Steve debuted in his family's show for a pie supper at his elementary school, singing "Walking the Floor Over You." Within a couple of years, he switched from vocalist to drummer—a role he fills today on the family's own stage.

BUILDING A DREAM

In 1967, Lloyd and Bessie Mae bought a ten-acre farm four miles from downtown Branson. The family took a leap of faith to build their dream—a metal box with a flat floor and double doors in the backside to adapt to Plan B: a boat storage business. The building accommodated 363 aging chairs purchased from the Shepherd of the Hills Outdoor Theatre. Occasionally, one of the weathered chairs collapsed under the weight of a guest.

The Presleys, except for the two older children, took up residence in the old farmhouse. Gary had married his high school sweetheart, Pat Adams, and they lived in a house trailer out back. A few days before the new theater opened, Deanna had married David Drennon, and they and his parents,

The Presleys' first sign on Highway 76. *Courtesy of the Presleys' Archives.*

Larry and Francis Drennon, were the original partners with Lloyd, Bessie Mae, Gary and Pat. June 30, 1967, marked the grand opening of Mountain Music Theatre. The words "Air Conditioned" took top billing on their sign. Admission: one dollar for adults and fifty cents for kids.

The entire family participated in the production—some onstage, others in the background. Lloyd played guitar and banjo. Gary performed as Herkimer. Sisters Deanna and Janice sang, and Deanna's husband David sang, played bass guitar and helped to emcee the show. Steve did double duty. During the show, he sat on a tree stump with a seat of plywood nailed to the top and kept rhythm on a snare drum. At intermission, he ran outside and stuck bumper stickers advertising the show on cars in the parking lot.

Within a year, the family remodeled the building and purchased more stable chairs from a church in Kansas. Their seating capacity increased to six hundred; ticket prices inched up to four dollars.

Steve remembers playing weeknight basketball through his junior high school. But high school games happened on Friday nights when the family played road shows during the winter months. He decided to drop basketball.

"All of the kids who've grown up with the show faced the same choices," Steve says, including his own children, his nephews and now a fourth generation of Presleys. "We were always given the choice to play on the show or do other things." However, like Steve, most have chosen the theater as a priority.

The Presleys were committed to their business—adults working day jobs and younger siblings, like Steve and Janice, cleaning the theater and selling advance tickets on summer days. Gary and Bessie Mae kept their jobs at the Royal Typewriter Company in Springfield. Pat found a job at a Branson bank, and Lloyd worked as a fishing guide on Taneycomo and Table Rock Lakes. After the first year, Larry Drennen sold his interest to the remaining Presleys, and a couple of years later, David and Deanna sold their interests. Within a few years, the Drennons established their own show, the long-running Pine Mountain Jamboree in Eureka Springs, Arkansas.

A Good Woman Behind Every Successful Man

In the case of the Presleys Mountain Jubilee, three good women stood behind Lloyd Presley and his sons, Gary and Steve. The late Bessie Mae Presley, matriarch of the family, admitted that the idea of a theater belonged to Lloyd. "But I went along with it because I love music—and Lloyd," she once said. While he picked a guitar night after night, she listened—and knitted.

Bessie Mae grew up with chores on her family's small farm in Alpena, Arkansas, in what she called an ordinary life. Duties and responsibilities remained throughout her adulthood, although she considered her jampacked "to do" list merely what a wife and mother does to serve her family and her God.

When the family moved to Branson to start their theater, Bessie Mae and Lloyd left behind a new house in Springfield. Bessie Mae described cracks in the floor of the old house on their new property big enough to see the ground underneath. Later, when they needed the farmhouse space to expand the theater, she and Lloyd moved into a mobile home. In 1973, they built two spacious houses—one for Lloyd and Bessie Mae and the other for Gary and Pat—behind the theater. Over the years, the family expanded the original theater seating from less than four hundred to its present two-thousand-seat capacity.

"We all worked hard and believed in our show," Gary says. "Mom found a day job in Branson at Chaney-Holman Gas Company. I remember her working all day, coming home and cooking supper before heading to the theater to sell tickets and concessions. After the show, she and Janice sewed on the entertainers' costumes. She also did all the bookkeeping and wrote checks for payroll and the bills."

Even after a Springfield seamstress started sewing costumes for the cast, Bessie Mae continued to make outlandish short-legged suits for comedian Sid Sharp, played by the late Windy Luttrell. Sometimes, she sewed shirts for Herkimer—bold prints with patch pockets—or smaller shirts for the "Little Herks."

From the beginning, Pat Presley worked a daytime job yet played an integral role in the theater. "Pat is the heart of the business office," Gary says. "Initially, she managed the box office, all ticket sales (including groups), bought merchandise for the gift shop, handled personnel matters and coordinated costumes—especially after we switched from the girls' gingham skirts and the guys' white shirts and string ties to fancy, sequined jackets and elegant dresses."

In 1976, Steve married his longtime sweetheart, Raeanne Miller, who had once ushered at the Presleys' theater. Immediately, she pitched in to help with theater operations, assisting Bessie Mae with bills and payroll and answering correspondence. Like other family members, she held a day job. Over the years—in addition to raising three children—Raeanne stepped into community roles, first serving as an alderwoman on the Branson City Council. She also served on the Missouri Tourism Commission, chaired the Springfield/Branson National Airport Board and sat as chairman of Skaggs Community Hospital in Branson.

Raeanne remains involved in the theater's business, often traveling to various conventions to promote tour bookings. Since 2007, she has served as mayor of Branson.

Today, three more women—including Malinda, wife of Scott, and Kelli, wife of Eric—join the forces behind their men onstage. Both young women manage ticket sales and assist Pat in overseeing the front of the theater. Nick's wife, Rhianna, helps out with the younger children who play backstage until it's time to dress in costume. Although Janice left the stage to raise her family, she sells the family's souvenirs and concessions.

The Presley performers acknowledge that audiences give *them* all the applause, but their women in the background taking care of business make their jobs onstage successful.

GROWING A MUSIC SHOW
ONE GENERATION AT A TIME

Today, four generations take the stage at Presleys' Mountain Music Jubilee. Scott, Greg and Eric, sons of Gary and Pat, started performing as soon as they toddled. Greg remembers family photos of him crawling on the stage.

The brothers recall playing in their front yard until about fifteen minutes before showtime. Their mother called them in, and they pulled on overalls that matched Herkimer's. After a song with their dad, they returned to the front yard—behind the theater—and played until time to sign autographs at the end of the show.

Scott remembers that once he forgot the words to his song. His mother filled a little tic-tac box with water and told him to sip it and he would never forget. "I did, and I never forgot my song again," he says. His brothers roll their eyes.

Now, Scott and Eric are both dads, watching fourth-generation Presleys balance childhood with a family music business. Scott, Greg and Eric, plus

Second, third and fourth generations of Presleys onstage at Presley's Country Jubilee. *Courtesy of Lee Smith.*

Steve's children, Nick, John and Sarah, all agree that they had options to follow a music refrain or pursue other interests. Often, they fit both tracks into their lifestyles. Growing up, Eric's passion—next to imitating Herkimer—centered on golf. He recalls that as a teenager, he did not go onstage until 9:00 p.m., allowing him time to linger after dark at the golf course. Sometimes, he arrived barely in time to pull his baggy overalls on over golfing slacks.

Greg remembers slipping into cowboy boots over his baseball stirrups. He still enjoys a baseball game. However, they all acknowledge that music is in their genes and that leaving the family show never entered their heads.

Scott plays lead guitar for his family's band, the harmonica is Greg's musical forte and Eric says that he copied his comedic genius from his dad. After all, he is Herkimer's son. However, he traded his carbon copy image in overalls and blackened teeth for a hillbilly who tries to appear educated. "Cecil has no idea that he doesn't have his life together," Eric says.

He dances with his knees tight, runs up stage walls, often swallows a balloon, rides a bicycle past the front row and crashes outside the door. His physical antics and hesitant monotone voice pitching upward at the end of a sentence keep the shows alive with laughter.

Nick, Steve and Raeanne's oldest son, took trumpet and violin lessons. He grew up playing guitar. Nick loves music, but he chose informational technology as a career. After graduating from California's Stanford University with a degree in communications, he returned to Branson and discovered his niche as video director for the family business. He also met his wife, Rhianna, and they have two children—adding to the fourth generation of Presleys.

At Presley's Country Jubilee, "Cecil" juggles on a stringed bass, strummed by "Herkimer" and family patriarch, Lloyd Presley. *Courtesy of Lee Smith.*

Steve and Raeanne's second child, John, started performing on the Presley stage at age ten. His Floyd Cramer piano style flows from the keys, but his infectious smile and dancing eyes win over his audience. In 2008, he married Ambrus Leigh, a lead vocalist on the show. They have one child.

Sarah, the youngest of the third generation and Steve and Raeanne's only daughter, decided at age eight to take up the violin. She began performing with the family two years later.

"Growing up in a theater is somewhat surreal and quite hard to explain to people who have never been to Branson," Sarah says. As she studies for a music business degree at Belmont University, Nashville, Tennessee, she often has to describe to others her unique background in a musical family.

"I feel very fortunate to have been born a Presley and to have such a rich family heritage," she continues. "The theater gave me something different and exciting to do as I grew up."

In high school, Sarah participated in the marching and jazz bands, learning to play the saxophone. Like all other Presley offspring, playing onstage was—and is—an option. However, like her cousins before her, she liked performing and earning a paycheck. Once, her cousin, Scott, who happened to be about Sarah's current age at the time, said, "I love entertaining so much I'd do it for free—but don't tell my parents!"

A Dog's Life

The Presleys love dogs. Pat and Gary raised and showed golden retrievers, and Pat trained German shepherds. Greg picked up that dog lover gene from his mom. His boxer, Albert, runs free in the theater during rehearsals, much as he and his two teenaged brothers once did when they played hide-and-seek in the darkened auditorium. John owns two Italian greyhounds. Adding a dog to their show made perfect sense. Biscuit, the huggable, man-sized dog, once paraded around the theater before the show and at intermission, striking high-fives with kids and posing for photos. He came on the scene after Scott was too big for the costume, but Greg and Eric took turns playing Biscuit. Next came their cousins Nick and John.

"I've heard John and Nick argue over who *got* to be the dog, and I've heard them argue over who *didn't* get to be the dog," Eric says. With another generation of Presley cousins coming on in the backstage playroom, someone is bound to grow into Biscuit's fur again.

Four generations of Presleys perform on their stage today. *Courtesy of Presleys' Country Jubilee Theater.*

THE PRESLEYS PRACTICE WHAT THEY PLAY AND PLAY WHAT THEY PRACTICE

This close-knit family has spent most of every day together for half a century—practicing, performing, making corporate decisions and even vacationing.

"There is no 'I' in Presley," Eric says. "From putting the show together to what you see on the billboards or what kind of candy we put in the snack bar, every decision on the hillside is discussed. It takes all of us to make it work."

In one remodel, the family gathered to decide on wallpaper for the lobby. They chose a stripe that looked subtle in the sample book. However, when it went up on the walls, one by one, each Presley said to another: "That makes me dizzy!" The wallpaper came down.

Built on the strong foundation laid by Lloyd and Bessie Mae, the cohesive family continues to work and play together. "And we never had to open the boat storage business," Lloyd says with a chuckle.

Chapter 8

The Working Man's Broadway

[Branson]…where you can take any member of the family in any show or attraction and not be embarrassed with the content.
—the late Lou Shaefer, Branson's first ambassador, who served as mayor from 1995 to 2007

In 1991, CBS's *Sixty Minutes* broke the story about a small town with a musical heart. Overnight, Branson changed from a dot on the Missouri map to a family vacation destination known as the "Live Music Show Capital of America." In Branson—a hometown environment—Broadway-quality entertainment became accessible to America's working man and his family.

However, Ed Anderson, founder and former publisher of *Branson's Review*, states: "Branson didn't just happen because of a twenty-minute spot on a news show. If you look really hard down 76 Country Boulevard, you'll see a lot of blood, sweat and tears. Those three commodities are from the local people who helped build this place into what it is today. They are the unsung heroes of the Ozarks."

Anderson referred to folks like the Herschends, the Trimbles, the Mabes and the Presleys. He also pointed to Darrell and Rosie Plummer, Missouri farmers who had a vision of earning their living entertaining other families. They opened their theater in May 1973 on a spot along Highway 76 that had once hosted a music show in a tent. Their offspring, Randy and Melody, bought into their parents' dream. The whole family, plus musicians they hired, pitched in to put out brochures, clean the theater, sell tickets and park cars. Families like the Plummers, the Presleys and the Mabes set the standard high for others who brought their talents to town.

The Foggy River Boys moved their music show to Branson in 1974. Formed in the tradition of the famous Jordanaires quartet of *Grand Ole Opry* fame, the original members, Bob Hubbard, Denzel Koontz, John Shepherd, Dale Sullens and Bob Moskop, were regulars on Springfield's *Ozark Jubilee*. Their harmonies in barbershop, gospel, country and pop tunes spread a slice of Americana in Branson. The group retired their act in 2002, except for occasional concerts.

Bob-O-Links, a new theater started by Bob Mabe, a founding member of the Baldknobbers, featured the Rex Burdette Family—the first dancers on Branson's stages. Later, Mabe partnered with a quartet, the Texans, to become the *Texans/Bob-O-Link Show.*

Four singing sisters headlined at the Lowe Family Theater on what had become known as "The Strip." The Lester Family and the Sons of the Pioneers also performed on their stage. Brothers named Wilkinson opened next door. The television show *Hee Haw* came to town, bringing their country music and comedy stars.

Starlite Theatre, owned and produced by Chisai Childs, opened avenues for acts that later became marquee names in Branson. Known for her sense of production, Childs introduced the numerous glitzy costume changes that happen on stages today.

In the early 1970s, mega country stars Dolly Parton, Buck Trent and Porter Wagoner had made guest appearances in a few theaters. Still, beyond the states bordering Missouri, Branson remained a well-kept entertainment secret.

Tourism stayed steady into the 1980s, but 1983 marked a tremendous growth spurt. The Braschler Family stormed stages at several theaters before building their own on Shepherd of the Hills Expressway. Terry Sanders, a daytime character actor on Silver Dollar City's streets, created laughs for Braschlers's nighttime audiences. Soon other family variety shows, such as Campbell's Ozark Country Jubilee and the 76 Music Hall, opened their doors. A group of youngsters, the Texas Gold Minors, performed in Campbell's theater. These shows, along with the established shows of the Presleys, Baldknobbers, Plummers, Bob-O-Links and the Foggy River Boys, built a foundation for Branson's music industry.

Stars Hitch Their Wagons to Branson

Observing the success of *Hee Haw*'s performances, Roy Clark and businessman Jim Thomas partnered to build the Roy Clark Theatre. While Clark made regular appearances, he introduced major recording stars to Branson's hometown atmosphere and started a trend of dozens of stars opening their own venues. By 1987, BoxCar Willie permanently located in a theater along Highway 76. Jim Stafford and his wife Annie took over their theater—and their place in Branson's community—in 1988.

"To have a theater in Branson is a dream come true," Stafford says. "There's a goodness in this area that's hard to describe. And there's a goodness in the visitors attracted to Branson."

Jim Stafford coined "musicomedy" to describe his show. "I intended to be a serious musician," he says. "I don't regret my hard work on the guitar. But I didn't have confidence in my singing voice, so I started writing musical parodies. I also honed talking to crowds and working in jokes and stories I had learned growing up in a rural Florida town."

Often acclaimed as the "Victor Borge of the Guitar," Stafford combines his skills with perfectly timed comedy—ball fringe dropping from a Mexican sombrero as he plays "Malagueña" or a smashed guitar he magically restores with duct tape. Dubbed "Gentleman Jim" by his friends, Stafford notes that his intimate 1,100-seat theater suits his style. His wife Annie runs the business. Before shows, she might be in the ticket booth and at intermission, scooping popcorn into

Internationally known entertainer Roy Clark. *Courtesy of Branson/Lakes Area Chamber of Commerce and Convention and Visitors Bureau.*

Master of musicomedy Jim Stafford. *Courtesy of Lee Smith.*

boxes. In recent years, the Staffords' son Shea and daughter G.G. joined their dad onstage— each a proficient musician and entertainer. Their family continues the tradition: families entertaining families.

THE 1900S BOOM

Veteran performers stated they had never seen a year that came close to the changes occurring at the beginning of the 1990s. Names like Mickey Gilley, Barbara Fairchild, Moe Bandy, Buck Trent, Ray Stevens and Mel Tillis flashed on theater marquees. Stars from outside the country music scene like Bobby Vinton, Andy Williams, John Davidson, the Osmonds, the Lennons and JoAnn Castle joined BoxCar Willie, Roy Clark and Jim Stafford to make their homes in Branson. Others dropped in for select dates: Barbara Mandrell, the Gatlins, the Oak Ridge Boys, Porter Wagoner, Louise Mandrell, Brenda Lee, Willie Nelson, John Denver, Reba McEntire, Charley Pride, Jimmy Rodgers, Lee Greenwood, Dino Kartsonakis and Loretta Lynn.

Like musical chairs, entertainers moved from theater to theater in different seasons. In the early 1990s, total makeovers and name changes happened. Christy Lane bought the Starlite. *Hee Haw's* stage turned into Country Music World—owned by the late Bill Dailey and wife, Janet, a bestselling novelist. Branson's season expanded to include Christmas lights and special shows, transforming the Ozarks into a gift-wrapped holiday world in November and December.

By that time, famous faces appeared regularly on Branson's stages. Magazines such as *Time* and *People* and newspapers such as the *Wall Street Journal* touted their "discovery" of quality entertainment in a small southwest Missouri town. When CBS showcased Branson on national television, the town had fewer than two dozen theaters. Some of the original family variety shows kept pace with new technology in stage lighting and sound. Others sold their theaters as celebrity names took over marquees. Moe Bandy turned the Plummer family's stage into the Americana Theatre. Mickey Gilley's theater rose on the spot garnered by Country Music World. Ray Stevens built his theater at the base of Dewey Bald, a mountain made famous in Wright's *Shepherd of the Hills* novel. Stevens stepped up the trend for production numbers, enhancing his comedy songs with a white Harley roaring across his stage.

Yet, even Stevens himself cannot explain why people clap like crazy when he pants like a dog, imitating an obscene phone-calling pervert—or how fans beyond southern boundaries understand when he talks about "minner buckets." However, he definitely understands his love for entertaining folks with his songs about a Shriners' convention and an Arab named Ahab.

WHY BRANSON?

Dan Lennon, vice-president of marketing for the Branson/Lakes Area Chamber of Commerce and Convention and Visitors Bureau, considers the changes in the 1990s decade. "The 'big names' who came to Branson had starred on television variety shows," he says. "That's critical to understanding what happened. At that time, television appeared warm and friendly. These people were in everybody's living rooms on a weekly basis."

"When they opened in Branson, folks came from everywhere to see stars they felt they knew personally," he continues. "With the lack of security, which is unnecessary in Branson, the performers came out after a show, posed for pictures, hugged fans and signed autographs. This is unheard of in Las Vegas or on Broadway."

Indeed, Branson changed and evolved during the 1980s and 1990s. However, the more things changed, the more they stayed the same—families entertaining families.

CHAPTER 9

A Fiddlin' Classic

From Japan to the Ozarks

I never picked cotton and my family never picked cotton. But I can fiddle up "Those Old Cotton Fields Back Home."

—*Shoji Tabuchi*

Shoji Tabuchi, the country fiddler with classical "licks" and a Japanese accent, tucks a fiddle under his chin, draws his bow across the strings and pulls an audience under his spell. From the stage of his luxurious theater reminiscent of the grand playhouse palaces of the 1930s, the master violinist intertwines classic melodies with foot-stomping renditions of "Orange Blossom Special," jazzy versions of "Autumn Leaves" and haunting refrains of "Through the Eyes of Love" from the movie *Ice Castles*.

The road bringing Shoji Tabuchi to the stages of America—and Branson, Missouri, in particular—began in Daishji, Japan, where he studied the Suzuki method of violin at age seven. Although his family background is comparable to America's upper-middle class today, both of his parents made sure that he and his siblings knew the value of working to attain the best in life.

"In Japan, if you don't work to achieve in studies, the arts and sports, you will be left behind. My mom pushed me to play the violin," he says with his animated grin. He goes on to admit that "I didn't like it when I was eight years old, and I'd see other kids playing around. But Mom made sure I had a violin in my hands at least twice a day."

Although by age thirteen Shoji showed musical promise, neither he nor his family ever thought of making music a career. Just as singing and plucking homemade instruments were diversions from work for Ozarks hill folks, Japanese people expected their children to develop interests to enrich a preprogrammed lifestyle in the Japanese workforce.

Shoji never thought about deviating from his parents' plan for him to complete college and follow his dad's footsteps into the corporate world. He entered St. Andrew's University in Osaka, Japan, and set his goal toward a major in economics. His musical studies were merely elective classes.

A Mockingbird Changes Life's Course

"In Japan, the competition between children and society is different from the United States," Shoji describes with his Japanese inflection. "Probably because Japan has many people on much less land."

However, in his sophomore year, the late Roy Acuff, longtime member of the *Grand Ole Opry*, performed a concert on the St. Andrew's University campus. Out of curiosity, Shoji sat in the audience.

"When Howdy Forrester played a song called 'Listen to the Mockingbird,' the chirping bird sounds coming from his instrument were different from anything I'd ever heard," he remembers. "I fell in love with country music at that concert."

Backstage, Shoji shared his newfound enthusiasm for their music with Roy Acuff and his band members. "If you ever come to the United States, look me up," Acuff told him.

"So my dream began—getting to the United States, seeing the *Grand Ole Opry* and the *Louisiana Hayride*," Shoji says, his dark eyes expressing the depth of his commitment to country music—an allegiance he did not share with his parents.

However, in Japan, he found other musicians interested in the same type of music. In his remaining college years, he joined a band called Bluegrass Ramblers. In contests with other country bands, they gained recognition.

By graduation time, Shoji stood at a crossroads in life. He could take a chance on his dream of becoming an entertainer, or he could step into the job waiting for him with a Japanese corporation. His dad happened to be in Thailand on business. Shoji persuaded his mother to launch his dream with $500 pocket money and another $100 tucked inside his shoe.

His mother said, "If this is what you want, Shoji, I'll accept your college diploma and explain to your dad." Her explanation fell on deaf ears. Shoji's dad considered his son's trek to the United States to be folly and refused to write to him for almost a year.

"It worked out fine," Shoji relates. "My parents visited us in America and were proud of me. But they were so practical, and their life was so different. They never understood that Americans switch jobs. And when we served them steak, they thought we were wasting money. The price of steak in Japan makes it a food only for the rich."

Shoji's first glimpse of American life began in San Francisco, where he and two Japanese friends formed a group called the Osaka Okies. He later left the West Coast for the plains of Kansas, where he again met Roy Acuff on tour. Acuff invited him to Nashville and promised Shoji a spot on the *Grand Ole Opry*.

He took the country music icon at his word and the following week drove straight to Nashville. On the Friday night *Opry* in the old Ryman Auditorium, Shoji fiddled his way into the hearts of country music fans—who gave him two standing ovations. His Nashville exposure paid off with an offer to join David Houston and the Persuaders. For five years, he toured major cities and performed with top names in the music industry.

SHOJI'S ROADSHOWS END AT BRANSON

"I was pretty much tired of touring and one-night stands," Shoji says. When show producer Chisai Childs, owner of a theater in Branson, invited him to

play a six-month season in one place, Shoji took a good look at the opportunity.

"Returning from a concert date in Illinois, I drove by this Branson. I couldn't believe it! Such a neat town with friendly people. I fell in love all over again."

Joining the cast at Starlite Theatre, Shoji played several seasons before moving to the stage of Country Music World. Night after night, he performed his wizardry on the violin strings, building a reputation among fans, who named him Instrumentalist of the Year in the Ozark Music Awards show for three consecutive years and Entertainer of the Year for 1984.

The Incredible Shoji Tabuchi.
Courtesy of Shoji Tabuchi Theatre.

Dorothy Tabuchi Steppin' Up

By Shoji's side in Branson, his wife and partner Dorothy gathered ideas and fanned the fire of their dream to perform in their own theater. She learned to book off-season concerts, promote her husband's talent and handle fan mail. In 1989, the time turned right for the Tabuchis to step out with a show all their own. Shoji confidently turned all production responsibilities over to Dorothy, who set to work to show off and stage Shoji's music with sets, costumes and a cast of performers who added a new dimension to entertainment in the Ozarks.

"Shoji's satisfaction comes from giving his best performance onstage," Dorothy says. "My satisfaction comes from seeing the finished performance incorporated with my ideas."

At first glance, the Tabuchis are unlikely partners—worlds apart in background, culture and even language. Shoji—dark-skinned with jet-black hair framing his smiling face and taller than most Japanese—makes a sharp contrast to his petite blond wife. Nonetheless, from the moment they met, love at first sight took over, bonding a winning team in both business and home life.

Growing up in a close-knit Louisiana family, Dorothy's bubbly personality won her leadership roles in school clubs and cheerleading activities. Her ambitions for college with a major in journalism took a detour, with marriage following high school graduation. For the next eight years, she immersed herself in church and community affairs while nurturing her two youngsters, Christina and Jason. When the marriage ended, she coped with single parenthood by developing a newfound interest in voice and piano.

However, singing in church and a short six-month stint as a secretary offered little preparation when she stepped into the world of entertainment as the wife of a classical violinist—one who left his native Japan to fiddle country music on American stages.

"From the first day together, Shoji and I have worked as equal partners on everything that concerns his career," Dorothy says. "I adjusted to evenings behind stage at the concerts and hours of unwinding at home afterward. For many years, while most people slept, we did laundry, cooking and other chores. Then when 'regular folks' took a lunch break, we had breakfast. However, spending most daytime hours with the children made up for a crazy schedule."

Dorothy's presence backstage night after night put her in sync with Shoji's music and the audiences who applauded him. When the Tabuchis put together their show, Dorothy remembers taking a winter vacation to Caribbean beaches and lugging along a suitcase packed with music tapes—inspiration for production numbers.

"I've always done a lot of research for the right music," Dorothy says. "I know what I expect when I'm sitting in an audience, so I want our show to be magical and fun."

Initially, Dorothy acted as emcee, announcing "The incredible Shoji Tabuchi!" She also danced and performed a few songs. However, production duties quickly took her from the stage and into meetings concerning costume design, sets and choreography.

THE OZARKS VERSUS JAPAN

Settling into a home on a wooded hillside outside Branson, Shoji compares his Ozarks lifestyle to the one he left behind in Japan. "In Japan, you know, you take off your shoes." He holds up two stocking feet for emphasis.

Dorothy laughs. "But Shoji, going barefoot has been the custom forever in these hills!"

He agrees but continues comparing his two homes. "I'm not the type to get homesick. I do miss my family. But as far as missing the food or customs, I do not."

"You see, I gave myself inside-out to the country lifestyle," he continues. "I love the wide-open spaces. It's so different here from Japan, a country the size of California with many more times population. In Japan, every day you get on a train to go to work. There is one person whose job is just to push people into the train. Everywhere you look there are people."

In contrast to the Japanese train, Shoji drives a typical American pickup truck to the theater or to his favorite fishing hole or golf course. He even makes a joke on stage about one of his fellow musicians, who drives a Toyota. "I drive full-sized Chevrolet," he says, grinning at his own joke.

When Shoji arrived in the Ozarks, he went "crazy" over bass fishing on Table Rock Lake. "I used to go out with one of my favorite fishing partners, Lloyd Presley," he says. "He earned the title 'the Ozarks Fisherman,' and I learned from him."

His love of the sport carried into bits of ad-lib in his stage productions. Whether in western attire or a tuxedo, Shoji appears impeccable onstage. In one of his numerous flashy sequined jackets, he often performs fancy fiddling, ending up on his back, his fiddle high over legs curled above his torso. Without missing a musical note in his performance, he often bounces up and says, "Don't want to mess up my suit! Took whole year of fishing to get scales for this jacket!"

Shoji's spontaneity and wit further endears his performances to fans. His fishing buddy Lloyd Presley speaks to the fiddler's contribution to Branson's music industry: "Shoji is respected in the community for his high standards of musical entertainment. Along with his unmatched instrumental performances, he never forgets that his primary goal is to entertain, always keeping himself on the same level as his audience."

From Japanese to English

Shoji studied English in Japan, yet when he first arrived in the United States, the rapid speech of Americans made comprehension difficult. He often teases from his stage, "Bet you thought I couldn't speak English!"

Through his struggles and halting phrases, he has become more comfortable with the language. Dorothy relates that early on as they traveled by car on tours, she helped him with phrasing and wording on vocals. "I have to admit that I would be mad at her," Shoji says. "I'd say, 'Dorothy, you were born here. You know these things.'"

"Few people understand what it's like to hear a song and then have to interpret the meaning of the words and the phrasing before singing it," Dorothy explains. "Shoji has a wonderful voice, but for so many years, he only concentrated on the violin. Singing comes easier to him now—and he sings more in the show."

A Rising Star

The Shoji Tabuchi Theatre is a family affair. Christina Tabuchi started dance lessons at age three. By first grade, she stepped into the spotlight on her dad's segment of the show at Country Music World. When the Tabuchi family moved into their own theater, nine-year-old Christina became a featured vocalist and entertainer. During her growing years, she continued lessons in singing, dance and drama while performing in production numbers at their theater. With more than four hundred shows annually, entertaining two thousand guests per show, she had a lifetime of stage experience by age twenty.

For most of her education, Christina worked with tutors in her own designated apartment at the theater, an addition designed particularly for

Christina Tabuchi onstage in the Tabuchi Theatre in Branson. *Courtesy of Shoji Tabuchi Theatre.*

her schooling. She attended Branson High School during her senior year.

During high school, Christina made student trips to France and Japan, staying with host families. In France, she says that she knew enough language to order her food. However, despite growing up with a Japanese dad, she knew none of the language in Japan. "Dad always spoke English at home," she says. "He only spoke Japanese on the phone when he talked to family and friends."

However, on the trip, Christina picked up a bit of the language, and she could exchange phrases with her dad in Japanese. "He was so excited," she says. "We'd have to tell Mom what we were talking about."

Although Christina now resides in Nashville, Tennessee, she continues to perform on select dates at her family's elaborate theater in Branson. She also acts as vocal director and dance cocaptain for the show.

A WIDE SPECTRUM OF MUSIC

Although country music drew Shoji Tabuchi to the United States, his show in Branson covers all styles of music, from classical, Broadway and movie themes to country, western swing, rock and roll and gospel. His virtuoso performances and showmanship keep audiences returning year after year.

With his sense of musical perfection, Shoji selects professional musicians to form his orchestra. At every performance, he proudly announces that each musician behind him has a degree in music. He laughs when he points to himself and says, "I have degree in economics!"

The dancers fall under both Dorothy's and Christina's domain. A renowned choreographer and long hours of rehearsals result in a versatile dance company that adapts to numerous styles and productions onstage. Their creativity ranges from dancing with twirling cowboy ropes to lively polkas to the "Sugar Plum Fairy" danced on toe during a special Christmas performance. The company's extraordinary vocalists exemplify Broadway quality with lovely ballads, songs of the 1950s and 1960s and gospel hymns.

Although Shoji Tabuchi has never produced a recording on a major label, he ranks among the most popular musicians in the United States. A large number of his loyal fans arrive at his lavish theater in tour buses from across the nation.

A PERMANENTLY PLANTED SHOWPLACE IN THE OZARKS

The Shoji Tabuchi Theatre on Shepherd of the Hills Expressway complements Shoji's perfection in musical production—down to the ladies' and men's "necessary" rooms. All of Branson buzzed about the stunning million-dollar ladies' room back in the early 1990s. A few years later, the Tabuchis stirred even more talk around town with a billiard table and stately leather chairs in the men's room. Dorothy's inspiration came from her desire to entertain their guests from the moment they step onto the parking lot until they return to their transportation after the show.

The Tabuchis' zest for life, their commitment to a family-oriented show and their interest in the Ozarks culture blends them into the mainstream of country living in Branson. Although many people shake Shoji's hand after the show and tell him that he should be in Nashville, he smilingly responds, "I've been to Nashville; I performed twenty-eight times on the *Grand Ole Opry*. Branson actually has more talent in one small town than anywhere else in the world. I believe I can do anything I want with my career from here."

He goes on to say, "If I'm ever to make my name truly a household word, I'll have to go back to road tours. I don't know if I would trade that for the thousands of people who come from many states and countries to hear me while I stay in one place."

Shoji Tabuchi may not consider his name commonly spoken in most American homes, but he was invited to perform at the White House for a state dinner with former Japanese prime minister Junichiro Koizumi. The Missouri House of Representatives also honored him with the Outstanding Missourian Award. In the nation's house and in Missouri's House, his name is recognized.

CHAPTER 10

GROWING AN ACT
ONE FIDDLER AT A TIME

As a little boy living in Israel, Itzhak Perlman listened to classical violin music on the radio and longed to play the instrument. In his career as a famous violinist, he performed on Sesame Street and inspired another little boy living in Texas to take up the violin.

Imagine growing up with a one-hundred-acre theme park for a backyard playground: riding the fast tracks of a high-rising roller coaster, splashing in cool water on a log flume, swirling in an oversized barrel down a raging river and slurping slushy lemonades for a midday snack. Back in 1993, eight kids named Haygood considered it all in a day's work.

Maintaining a strict daily performance schedule at Silver Dollar City, however, involved more than the fun of theme park rides. The Haygood Family Fiddlers broke ground of a different kind from the early settlers coming into the isolated Ozark Mountains. While hill folks whacked away brush to follow trails along rock ledges, the Haygoods, headed by parents Jim and Marie, followed a well-traveled highway from their too-small mobile home in Texas to Branson's mushrooming music industry. Invited to play a three-month contract at Silver Dollar City, dad Jim drove the six performing brothers, a toddler sister and baby Aaron in his mother's arms in a dilapidated twelve-seat van purchased at a government auction. Like their pioneering predecessors, they carried meager possessions, their fiddles and equal measures of courage and faith.

"We weren't sure what we'd do beyond the summer season at Silver Dollar City," Marie Haygood recalls. "But we knew in our hearts we were supposed to move to Branson."

The Beginning: Itzhak Perlman, a Violin and Sesame Street

The petite mother of eight remembers the beginning of the musical adventure that became a full-time family career. Influenced by Itzhak Perlman's first appearance on *Sesame Street*, five-year-old Timothy waged a compelling campaign for violin lessons. One by one, the Haygoods enrolled their children in the Suzuki method, except for Patrick—who opted to learn keyboards. The younger boys, Dominic, Shawn, Michael and Matthew, drew bows across violin strings, copying their older brother. Because the Suzuki method requires a parent to practice daily with the child, Marie's hours of listening to violin exercises swirled into full days.

She remembers the night Jim came home from work at 9:00 p.m., and she was still practicing with the fourth child. There was no dinner. He announced that from then on, he would shop and make dinner. Marie whispered, "Good!"

Jim adds, "Professor Suzuki believed a family that bonds together through music becomes a strong unit. I'm convinced that our children, now grown, will pick up a fiddle and somewhere in their hearts have warm fuzzy feelings because of all the hours spent with their mom behind a door—closed to the madness of our large household."

Fiddles, Festivals and Fairs

As a young adult, Jim had stormed a few stages in acting roles. But entertainment never topped his list of goals. Marie had danced in school musicals and participated in acting, vocal and piano lessons. She was cast in a few professional shows in Hawaii. But once the oldest of ten siblings married, her focus centered on motherhood. Indeed, neither parent imagined that their offspring would form a family band.

Yet Marie firmly believed that God called her to support their children in honing their musical talents. "I remember one day in my kitchen telling God that I would dedicate my life to mold each one into a well-rounded musician who would never want for a job," she says. "I asked only one thing in return—that I would lose none of my children to vanity."

"To accomplish this goal, Jim and I determined we didn't need *things*. We scraped together pennies for lessons and travel," she continues. "We drove in beat-up old cars to their performance dates and sat on bales of hay while the children fiddled at fairs and festivals around our hometown of Boerne, Texas."

Marie admits that they were smitten. "Here we had a little act!" she says. "I never regretted one moment—not even those long, long hours in the Texas heat."

As time went on, more festivals requested their act. While performing in the Children's Barn at the San Antonio Rodeo, a couple booked the family fiddlers for their anniversary party. "They asked about our fee," Marie remembers. "We knew nothing about fees! We were happy to use our God-given talent. But we charged them a whole twenty-five dollars!"

Bookings increased, along with their charges. "To our joy, people paid and continued to ask for the kids," she continues. "We added four band members. A lady made vests for the boys, and I started coordinating numbers and costumes. With each performance, we polished our routine."

By age twelve, Timothy had progressed from lessons to a featured spot onstage with Fiddlin' Frenchie Burke, a well-known Cajun-style fiddler in Texas and Louisiana. The younger boys picked up their brother's tunes and often played at nursing homes and local events.

Their schedule snowballed. Every Saturday, Jim packed his family, six fiddles, a keyboard and several speakers into their van. Performing in and around San Antonio for the rewards of free rides at a fair or food coupons at a festival, the tightly knit brothers hopped from one Texas town to another until Sunday night. Jim notes that the small compensation gave value to the boys' hard work in lessons and practice.

From Boerne to Branson

From the beginning, Jim and Marie had ordered their priorities into a motto: "Faith, Family, Freedom."

"Yet we pondered how we could raise a decent family in a world that feels like a cat chasing its tail. We believed our children needed constant supervision," Jim goes on. "The opportunity to perform at Silver Dollar City provided a way for us to be together every day."

The Haygood youngsters fiddled, tap-danced, harmonized and spun a few rope tricks straight into the hearts of audiences at the family-oriented theme park. For the first season, they entertained in the city's Gazebo—outdoors with no shade.

The Haygoods performing at Silver Dollar City. *Courtesy of Arline Chandler.*

Silver Dollar City extended their contract through Christmas and the following year. The third year, the young fiddlers progressed to the Boatworks Theater and an air-conditioned dressing room to accommodate their home-schooling schedule. "It was like progressing from VIP bracelets for free rides at a Texas fair to free rides *plus* food coupons," Jim states. "We Americans teach that hard work pays off. Our kids experienced it firsthand."

Behind those freshly scrubbed faces sporting genuine smiles on Silver Dollar City stages, fine-tuned teamwork challenged both parents and Haygood siblings. During the nine-month season of the city, Jim and Marie woke their children at 3:00 a.m. to dress, eat a hearty breakfast, warm up their act and load instruments and costumes into the car. In between five or six daily shows, babysitters whisked the two younger ones off to the petting zoo and carousel, while Jim and Marie supervised schooling and music practice. They also built in free time for the boys to roam the park, seeking out fun experiences and making friends.

"I don't know of any other kids who got to ride a roller coaster twelve times a day," Timothy quips today, looking back at their onstage training at Silver Dollar City.

Early on, the Haygood boys considered choosing their own lunch menu from the city's restaurants and food booths a working guy's perk. "We trusted

The young Haygoods in rehearsal at their home. Mother Marie is in charge. *Courtesy of Arline Chandler.*

them to select healthy food," Jim says. "Only once did we have to reign in Matthew when he spent his day's food allowance on cheesecake!"

"We were a different type of entertainment in the park," Marie adds. "To be taken seriously, we had to make inroads. Some people questioned why we put our children into entertainment."

"Over time, our dedication to their musical growth and well-being proved that we were not stage parents out to exploit their talents," she continues. "As each year's contract was negotiated, we had open, honest discussions about whether or not we were going to continue; do something else; or get on the big yellow school bus that passed our house each morning. At times, different ones announced they would quit. However, they understood that once they agreed to perform and their dad signed a contract, they were expected to follow through for that year."

Marie designed each season's show to include the budding talents of the two youngest Haygoods, Catherine and Aaron. With a laugh, she says that toddler Aaron performed only when his attitude was suitable for going onstage.

The young Haygoods at their home taking a break from rehearsals. *Courtesy of Arline Chandler.*

ON THE HAYGOOD HOMEFRONT

When all eight Haygood children lived at home, a handwritten schedule taped to their kitchen's refrigerator marked hourly slots scheduling meals, practices, rehearsals, performances, schooling, lessons, physical training and free time. A shorter roster designated which boys had dish duty. Everyone pitched in to clean, cook and do laundry. Even as a toddler, Aaron scrubbed the dining chair seats after a meal. Now that six of the eight siblings live on their own, they look back at the massive amount of self-discipline the whole family contributed to balance a home life with their rigid schedule.

After a day of performances—with school lessons squeezed into the hours—the Haygood kids arrived at their home in Kimberling City and sped off on dirt bikes or bicycles. Typically, Patrick tucked tiny Aaron inside his jacket. They swung from ropes knotted on tree limbs and played soccer or basketball with neighborhood buddies. However, Marie points out that the brothers also were friends with one another. They worked together yet they played together. They still do.

Growing up, their weekends typically happened on Monday and Tuesday throughout Silver Dollar City's operating schedule. On one of the days, the family did household chores, lessons and practices. The other day was totally devoted to play. Once, they rented the local roller rink for a Haygoods hockey game. On rainy days, they loaded the computers with video games. Often they rented a pontoon boat to motor across Table Rock Lake to their favorite island. Although all the boys talk about the size of the fish they caught, they remain tight-lipped even today about the exact spot for the "Haygood hole."

BACK AT THE CITY

The Haygoods—supported by a company that expressed a true desire to see the children grow musically—stepped up in location and professionalism each year. "Performing at Silver Dollar City was a great learning experience," Marie says, recalling that the company assigned a dance teacher and a full-time director to their show after the first two years. "We gained much—and we gave back to the park and its gracious audiences."

Over nine seasons at Silver Dollar City, the youngsters performed at almost every theater in the park—eventually claiming prime showtimes in the Opera House in 1999. By that time, eight-year-old Catherine and six-year-old Aaron matched steps, fiddle tunes and fine singing with their older siblings. Dad Jim described the show as a four-hundred-pound alligator that clamped on the audiences' legs—and held on for forty intense minutes.

"Their signature fiddle numbers pulled together a show that's contemporary yet traditional," Jim states. He points out his sons' acumen with a wide range of additional instruments: drums, electric and bass guitars, mandolin, acoustic guitar and saxophone. "While performing at the City, the boys' vocal harmonies grew stronger as they took advantage to learn from various performing groups. Their choreography and acrobatics matched their musical growth. Catherine became proficient on the harp and piano, as well as the saxophone. The plunk of a banjo often bounced around our home as Big Brother Timothy taught her a few licks."

Marie notes that Jim's carpenter skills on building projects at Silver Dollar City added to their income during the winter seasons:

The kids never felt they had to perform for the family's livelihood. They were driven by a desire to give back, by an eagerness to affect a generation of their own and a dream to make it to "the top." They've worked hard, but they enjoy what they are doing. Most youngsters never have such opportunities to develop their talents in this fashion. We were blessed with a unique setting at Silver Dollar City that provided income for our family and on-the-job training, as well.

Jim adds that over the years a couple of the children had offers to join other prestigious bands or acts. He points out that in 1995, the entire family, except for Patrick, took on roles of pioneers in *Ozarks, Legacy and Legend*, an IMAX film about the history, culture and beauty of the Missouri hills.

Dominic, cast as the orphan boy adopted by the McFarlains, played by Jim and Marie, rose to the challenge of his first speaking role. Timothy helped to direct the music in scenes with down-home fiddling. Aaron, a tiny two-year-old during filming, may today choose to deny that he is the bonneted "baby girl" his mother lulled to sleep on her shoulder.

From Silver Dollar City to Branson Town

In 2001, Jim and Marie determined to step back and let go of their family act. The older boys were living on their own; Timothy and Patrick both had married. They were taking over aspects of the family's music business. On May 10, 2002, the Haygoods opened a fast-paced, energetic show in their own theater at Music City Centre on Branson's famed 76 Country Boulevard. From backstage at each evening's performance, Jim and Marie watched their eight children come into their own roles in the music industry.

The Haygoods—Timothy, Patrick, Dominic, Shawn, Matthew, Michael, Catherine and Aaron—continue to fiddle, flip, pick, croon and kick up a few heels to deliver the high-energy performances their audiences expect. Appealing to every age group, they perform music from classical and country to rock and gospel. Their a cappella harmonies tug heartstrings. Their dance version of *Stomp!* invigorates the audience.

Ever moving toward their goal at the top of the showbiz industry, the Haygoods once again stepped out on faith in March 2009, opening their own venue, the New Americana Theatre. Following a $500,000 renovation—featuring state-of-the-art sound and effects, a spacious lobby and a gourmet deli—the Haygoods became the youngest family to own a theater on the Branson strip. Although the Haygoods headline the New Americana Theatre, they also feature other morning and afternoon shows—including Timothy's wife starring in *Cassandré: The Voice of an Angel.*

Cassandré Faimon-Haygood sings time-honored classics, popular tunes, gospel, Broadway and contemporary hits—backed by a live orchestra that includes Catherine Haygood. For nine years, Cassandré was featured in Silver Dollar City Opera House productions like *For the Glory, Dickens' Christmas Carol* and *Headin' West.*

The Haygoods all grown up. *Courtesy of the Haygoods.*

"We give credit to God's guidance for the development of our family's talent and productions," Marie Haygood says. "If it all ended tomorrow, our family has accomplished in less than two decades what many strive a lifetime to achieve. We blazed a new trail into the Ozarks' music scene, and we're blessed to have traveled that road together."

CHAPTER 11

THE BRANSON CONVERSION

Family values, loyalty, history, work ethic and tradition. Branson was built on these
words and the people who believed in them.
—Peter Herschend, cofounder of Silver Dollar City

L arry Welk, son of the late Lawrence Welk, had that 'Branson conversion'
that people describe," says Dan Lennon, one of the singing Lennon
Brothers. "He fell in love with the town and dubbed Branson a setting in
which to preserve the Welk musical legacy. He elected to build the Welk
complex, including a hotel, theater and restaurant. Larry asked my sisters
[the Lennons] if they would come to Branson and host the show."

In 1993, Dan Lennon and sisters Kathy and Janet and their husbands,
checked out the possibility of moving their families from Southern California
to southwest Missouri. "We talked to people who had made that switch—
John Davidson, the Osmonds, Andy Williams—people with whom our
family had shared stages," Lennon says. "We met some of the local folks—
the Presleys, the Herschends, the Baldknobbers."

Yet Lennon says he did not *get* what was happening in Branson until he
visited Jim Stafford's theater. "I wasn't into country music," he says, noting
that he grew up in a crowded coastal environment and often performed in
jazz clubs. "Suddenly I'm in this theater with nine hundred people and no
smoke in the air. Midwestern and southern folks surrounded me. I felt as
though I'd gone to a foreign country."

He explains that Jim Stafford came onstage strumming "You Are My
Sunshine" on his guitar. He invited his audience to sing along. People

laughed. He insisted. Soon everyone was singing. Jim remarked, "Now, wasn't that nice?"

"Such a simple, beautiful thing—all these people in this peaceful, clean environment singing 'You Are My Sunshine.' I thought—what an unusual place. Next, Jim asked, 'How many are here with your kids or grandkids? Hold them up!' Immediately, 150 kids were lifted above parents' and grandparents' heads," Lennon said. "And Jim continued, 'Now, *this* is what it's all about. These kids.' I sat there speechless…thinking…this is entertainment at its *best* in this town! I don't mean that Branson is a fairyland. But it's about simple music, children and things that deserve to be preserved in this world."

Dan Lennon and his sisters returned to California and called a family meeting. "There are eleven of us with wives, husbands and children—about one hundred in all. Twenty-nine chose to pull up roots in California and put new ones down in Missouri. We experienced the Branson conversion!"

The Lennons performed in the new Welk Champagne Theatre with other stars from television's *Lawrence Welk Show*. Three sisters, Janet, Kathy and Mimi, continue to stage a Christmas show with Tony Orlando. Until 2002, Dan Lennon, his brothers Joe and Bill and Bill's wife Gail started mornings off in the resort's restaurant with songs of the 1930s and 1940s.

Next they performed at Branson Mall for a year and then at Jim Stafford Theatre for a year. In 2004, the group did a Christmas season with Mickey Rooney. "Since that time, the market for our style of music has changed," Dan Lennon says. "We do five or six concerts a year for various groups and about a dozen seminars annually for Exploritas [formerly Elderhostel] here in Branson."

MANY STAKE A CLAIM, NOT ALL ARE "BRANSONIZED"

"When our family came—and we weren't the only ones—we were welcomed by the family businesses," Lennon continues. "We were invited to participate and then 'watched' to see if what we contributed made sense to the established values. When newcomers join the PTA, go to city council meetings, community cleanups and small-town events—over time, they are accepted into this magical place. Gary Presley calls it 'Bransonizing.' That's not a judgment on who stays or leaves, but some don't share the same values in terms of hard work, honesty, fairness and the fact that kids are important.

"We became part of the Branson community and enrolled our kids in the town's public schools," he says. "We are 'Bransonized!'"

Branson entertainers—Moe Bandy, the Lennons, Yakov, Andy Williams, the Osmonds and others—celebrate the opening of the Welk Theatre in Branson in 1994. *Courtesy of Dan Lennon.*

ANDY WILLIAMS CREATED HIS OWN MOON RIVER

Andy Williams had his Branson conversion without even as much as a booking to test the market. His brother, Don Williams, Ray Stevens's personal manager, insisted that Andy take a look at Branson.

"I spent two days in my car on Highway 76 between a Chevy truck and a camper," Williams jokes. "No traffic moved. Yet no one shouted or honked their horns. No one went for the gun rack behind the truck seat. Right then I decided to move to Branson!"

Sinking more than $11 million into a contemporary theater that anchors a parklike complex, Williams says his two-thousand-seat Moon River Theatre is the right size for him. "The sound and lighting are perfect; everyone in the audience can see the stage. The walls are a backdrop for my art collection. I've never been happier performing anywhere else," he says.

Andy Williams is considered an honorary local by those whose history traces to the beginning of the town. Dubbed "Mr. Christmas" due to his extravagant Christmas productions, he led the Christmas Parade of Stars in 2010.

Andy Williams, Branson's "Mr. Christmas." *Courtesy of Moon River Theatre.*

Growing up in Wall Lake, Iowa, Williams is no stranger to small-town values. His family's Presbyterian church choir first introduced him to music. Later, he and his brothers sang hymns on a radio show in Des Moines. During the 1960s, he signed with Columbia Records and recorded numerous hits, including his signature song, "Moon River."

His popularity as one of the world's greatest singers launched his successful NBC television series *The Andy Williams Show*. For nine years, he entertained in America's living rooms—endearing himself and his music to folks like the ones in his Iowa hometown. He brings those same songs to Branson audiences.

"Branson is a wonderful place to hang my hat, my golf clubs and my Minnie Pearl autographed picture," Williams said the first year he opened Moon River Theatre. Indeed, his hat and his heart are at home in Branson.

THE OSMONDS LISTENED TO FATHER

A family car trip to Yellowstone National Park started the Osmond brothers harmonizing. Father George began singing "The Old Oaken Bucket," and before the family arrived at their destination, the four brothers, Alan, Wayne, Merrill and Jay, were joining in harmony. The late George and Olive Osmond were the boys' first teachers, and the Osmond grandparents made up their first audience. In 1962, Andy Williams introduced the Osmonds to America on national television. From that point, the musical talents of the four brothers, plus Jimmy, Donny and Marie, became household names.

After forty years of touring and successful runs on television in *The Donny and Marie Show* and *The Osmond Family Show*, brother Jimmy persuaded his siblings to star on their own stage in Branson. Their parents applauded the move and took seats for each show in their new theater. Following their move to Missouri, the late Olive Osmond said, "It's like a little bit of heaven for us to be here in Branson with our kids!"

Members of the Osmonds still make their home in Branson. Although the Osmond brothers continue to tour the United States and Europe, Jimmy Osmond notes the phenomenal support they have received from Branson audiences since they first opened their theater in the music city.

MEET BARBARA FAIRCHILD IN THE MORNING

Growing up on a northeast Arkansas farm, Barbara Fairchild immediately fit into Branson's culture when she brought her talent to town. Her stories of "fighting and scratching as one of three kids in my family" became her trademark, alongside her celebrated song, "I Wish I Was a Teddy Bear."

From her first performances at the Roy Clark Celebrity Theatre, and from later dates with *Grand Ole Opry* star Johnny Russell at the Lowes Theater, Fairchild admits that she fell head over heels in love with Branson and its people. "The town's openness to gospel music attracted me most," she says. "I love the family atmosphere and the small-town feel. And it's a safe place for children."

She performed on the Mel Tillis show and in her own morning show at the Jim Stafford Theatre. Currently, she and her husband, Roy Morris, host a morning show at her "dream come true" Barbara Fairchild Diner. "I love everybody from little ol' babies to folks 110," she says in her Arkansas drawl. "For me to meet and entertain people every morning and, perhaps, touch someone for God is a privilege!"

PUSHING THE ENVELOPE

"One of the reasons Branson has succeeded—even with all the changes in the last two decades—the 'product' stays the same," Dan Lennon states. "Entertainment pushes the envelope in terms of what's here—the Chinese Acrobats, Paul Revere and the Raiders, Liverpool Legends, the Moscow Circus, *The Legend of Kung Fu*, zip lines, water parks and museums such as the Titanic [Museum], Ripley's Believe It or Not! and the Veterans Memorial Museum. These things give the town incrementally more things to offer, but the product is still family entertainment."

Barber and Seville onstage. Jim Barber appears to trade places with Seville. *Courtesy of Jim Barber.*

During the 1990s, comedians, magicians and ventriloquists—namely Yakov Smirnoff, Jim Barber, Dave Hamner and Kirby VanBurch—fit into the community, making Branson their hometown. As a stand-up Russian comedian, Yakov Smirnoff first performed on cruise ships in the Black Sea.

"Americans were the most open, the most alive, the most daring, the most free," he recalls. He first glimpsed Lady Liberty in the New York Harbor in 1977, and he remembers her human quality of a woman embracing him—telling him everything would be all right. He worked hard to learn the English language and build a career as an entertainer. In 1993, Yakov began sharing his talents as a performer, producer, actor, columnist, artist and author with Branson's audiences. Most of all, he shares his pride in being an American—and an Ozarks—citizen.

Jim Barber's no dummy. But when his act, Barber and Seville, opens onstage, Seville's head bobs above the shoulders and arm that carries Barber's expressive face perched on the dummy's midget form. As a ventriloquist, he combines theatrical, musical and production skills to create his one-man show. Before making his home in Branson, Barber shared stages with a long list of big-name stars in Nashville—and on hundreds of college campuses across the nation.

He labels himself as an entertainer who incorporates ventriloquism in an act of singing, dancing and special effects. Barber merges performance with a career in multimedia. He says that Branson is a logical place for his family to establish roots.

Jim Barber partners with Dave and Denise Hamner in the *Hamner-Barber Variety Show*. The magical Hamners produce macaws and cockatoos that appear amid flying cards, flaming swords, falling coins and jewels.

After traveling around the world and dazzling crowds with his wild illusions, Kirby VanBurch came to Branson in 1992. He quickly fell in love with the Ozarks and the entertainment community. VanBurch made Branson his permanent home. Known as the Prince of Magic, his act involves the appearance of a thirty-five-foot JetRanger helicopter onstage. He is also known for a menagerie of animal friends as costars, including leopards, lions, a white Royal Bengal tiger named Branson and, reportedly, a unicorn.

AUTHENTIC CONNECTIONS

Dan Lennon says that the foundation laid by the hill folks, who were here when Marble Cave operated, created what the Branson/Lakes Area Chamber of Commerce and Convention and Visitors Bureau terms "authentic connections": "We conducted a study, asking 'Why the Ozarks? Why Branson?' Lots of places have beautiful lakes and hospitable people. Yet, there's something about the mountains, water, trails and trees in the Ozarks combined with the live entertainment bonanza—one hundred shows within a twenty-minute driving radius—that makes Branson unique."

"Visitors will not see casinos and strip clubs," he says. "Acts with 'gray area' kinds of entertainment simply do not succeed. They may be acceptable elsewhere. Local folks and visitors, however, do not patronize them in Branson."

Chapter 12

The World's Spotlight on Branson

Today, fifty theaters make Branson the country's live music show capital. Boasting more than fifty-seven thousand seats—more than Broadway, Las Vegas or Nashville, Tennessee—Branson, Missouri, attracts about eight million visitors annually.

Stutterin' Boy

Early in 1990, Mel, Mickey and Moe—as in Tillis, Gilley and Bandy—made Branson their hometown. Mel Tillis put out more than fifty-eight albums in a career now stretching more than half a century. Prior to establishing his own show and theater in Branson, he had played occasional bookings for twenty-two years with the Baldknobbers and the Bob-O-Links Theater. In the late 1980s, he frequented Roy Clark's new stage and a couple of the area's amphitheaters. When he made his move to Branson in 1990, he knew the audiences and saw potential in the small town.

Tillis brought his seventeen-member band and three of his five daughters, who helped run his theater and occasionally sang onstage. Daughter Pam, a big name in her own right, as well as his songwriter son Mel Jr., made special appearances with their dad.

The acclaimed entertainer acknowledges that songwriting has supported his family since the late 1950s. But like many other big names, his recordings took off once he had television exposure. "The fans saw the real Mel Tillis—stutter and all," he said. "The stutter was there. I couldn't get rid of it, so I capitalized on it!"

For more than a decade, Mel Tillis and his family entertained other families in his spacious, state-of-the-art theater. He remarks that fans expect him to sing his hits, such as "Detroit City" and "Ruby, Don't Take Your Love to Town," but in his theater he added dancers, special effects and different material. "I set a constant high standard for my band and cast," he says, noting that many members of his Statesiders Band have worked with him three decades or longer.

The Mel Tillis Theatre turned into the Tri-Lakes Center in 2002, but the self-described "stutterin' boy" continues to perform select dates in Branson. In 2007, he was inducted into the *Grand Ole Opry* and became a member of the Country Music Hall of Fame—the culmination of a lifelong dream. In April 2010, he received the Cliffie Stone Pioneer Award from the Academy of Country Music.

THE URBAN COWBOY

Over two decades ago, Mickey Gilley, the singer with a boogie-woogie beat, moved into his own theater—a spot formerly occupied by Country Music World. His interest in the community and his love of Ozarks people melded his urban cowboy image into a hometown Bransonite.

"Performing in Branson is the ultimate in my career," the self-made musician and businessman states. In his own theater, he controls the lights and sound. On a favorite grand piano, he pounds out his seventeen number one hits—the Gilley signature diamond rings flashing in a mirror reflecting the keyboard.

He admits a love for performing. "I can walk out on the stage in my own theater and feel a confidence I could not have if I was doing a fair date somewhere under the boiling sun. Branson is the ultimate as far as a lifestyle is concerned."

BANDY THE RODEO CLOWN

While Mickey Gilley earned his reputation as an urban cowboy in his famous Texas honky-tonk, Moe Bandy took his hits in the dirt of a rodeo arena. He first fell in love with Ozarks scenery when he played a rodeo near Branson. Repeated injuries took him off the bronc-riding circuit. While working on a Texas ranch, he started writing his songs. He and wife, Margaret, pawned their furniture in 1974 to pay for a recording session. Audiences liked his down-home persona and his rich, deep voice. In 1991, he brought his famous songs "Bandy the Rodeo Clown" and "Till I'm Too Old to Die Young" to his own Branson stage. "I'm all about entertaining folks," he says. "My show features my songs, other writers' songs and impersonations—whatever it takes to entertain."

BRANSON MADE ROOM FOR TONY, JOHN, WAYNE AND BOBBY

Entertainer Jim Stafford claims that "Branson is a place where fans sing along!" By 1993, folks were humming or tapping toes to "Tie a Yellow Ribbon Round the Ole Oak Tree," a song made famous by Tony Orlando. The energy bouncing between Orlando and his musicians caught the attention of jean-clad twenty-year-olds and polyester-suited seniors alike. Clapping and cheering fans sprang to their feet in his Yellow Ribbon Theatre.

Although Orlando closed his theater, he continues to make Branson his hometown. Over the years, his experiences—welcoming home POWs with his "Yellow Ribbon" song—inspired him to plan a tribute to servicemen and servicewomen. "The soil in Branson is fertile for the Yellow Ribbon Salute to Veterans each November 11," he says.

His specially produced extravaganza is free to servicemen and servicewomen and their families. As part of this salute, Orlando presents the Yellow Ribbon Medal of Freedom. While performing more than two thousand shows in Branson, he was named Branson's Entertainer and Vocalist of the Year in 1993 and 1998.

John Davidson, another newcomer to the Branson scene during the 1990s, hugged the ladies and shook the gents' hands as he sang, "In Branson, we can all be heroes or clowns." He summed up Branson in another verse: "I'm so glad you came to Branson 'cause it's a place where dreams come true... for families and folks like you."

Wayne Newton took up residence in a three-thousand-seat theater patterned like a Virginia mansion. His entertainment skills soon garnered him the name "Mr. Branson." Yet the title did not stick, and Newton returned to his former name, "Mr. Las Vegas."

Bobby Vinton's Blue Velvet Theatre brought the big-band era to Branson as he shared the headline with the Glenn Miller Orchestra. Vinton, who has sold more than seventy-five million recordings, said that he thought he had "died and gone to heaven" when he discovered Branson. However, like many of the stars who set up shop in the entertainment town during the "boom," Vinton now plays limited engagements.

THE GRAND PALACE

Kenny Rogers, famous for his hit song, "The Gambler," partnered with Silver Dollar City in 1992 and built the Grand Palace. Rogers made frequent appearances, but Glenn Campbell, Louise Mandrell and Barbara Mandrell also commanded the stage in summer seasons. For more than a decade, America's biggest names took their bows at the four-thousand-seat theater. The Radio City Rockettes made the Palace a Christmas tradition between 1994 and 2003. Yet the hope that artists would begin to say "I played the Palace" instead of "I played the *Grand Ole Opry*" did not happen.

ANNUAL CHRISTMAS EXTRAVAGANZA

During the 1990s, Dino Kartsonakis brought his Annual Christmas Extravaganza to town, setting his glittery grand piano on various stages over the last two decades. The virtuoso pianist plays a mixture of styles and arrangements, at times introducing musicians playing five grands in sync. Dino's wife, Cheryl, and a cast of dancers create a highly anticipated Christmas production.

Baking happens to be Dino's second-greatest passion—after music, of course. At his Branson home, he used to stir up delicious creations and invite his friends, Tony Orlando, Bobby Vinton and Daniel O'Donnell over for samples. They urged him to market his carrot cake. Cheryl encouraged Dino to venture into the business of baking. In 2007, 24Karrot Company opened in two locations, Branson and Hollister, Missouri. Dino calls his places "the Sweetest Spot in Town."

DINNER WITH SONG, DANCE AND PRANCING HOOVES

Every night since 1995 at Branson's Dixie Stampede, with its blue-blooded beaus and blushing belles, the South rises again. Not to be outdone, the North shows up favorably with its own lovely ladies and dashing gents. A

The Rockettes at the Grand Palace. *Courtesy of Silver Dollar City.*

Grand Parade at Dixie Stampede. *Courtesy of Dixie Stampede.*

feast—nary a fork in hand—is served in the midst of the friendly North-South rivalry played out with singing, dancing, buckboard races and trick riding. While the cowboys and cowgirls are graceful and talented, the sleek, fast-running horses are the stars.

Showboat's a'Comin'

The *Showboat Branson Belle*, steaming across Table Rock Lake a few miles from Branson, re-creates a period in history full of adventure and romance. Just as the century-old "floating palaces" brought big city entertainment to isolated farmers, loggers and storekeepers, the opulent showboat stirs the imagination of today's generation.

Christened on April 13, 1995, the largest paddle-wheel steamboat in the United States on a landlocked lake fits into Branson's family-oriented entertainment scene. The football field–sized boat is totally committed to wholesome entertainment appealing to all ages.

While designers achieved historically accurate detailing in the *Showboat Branson Belle*'s construction and styling, the 265-foot-long vessel is larger than

The *Showboat Branson Belle* at sunset on Table Rock Lake. *Courtesy of Silver Dollar City.*

Todd Oliver and friends headline entertainment on the *Showboat Branson Belle*. *Courtesy of Silver Dollar City.*

the 1880s showboats that once plied North American rivers—including the White River at Branson. Resembling a century-old opera house, the dinner theater's three-tiered atrium, with balconies wrapping three sides of the ship and facing the stage, guarantees a good vantage point from any table. For thirteen seasons, a fast-paced musical revue with the comedy of ventriloquist Todd Oliver and his talking dogs entertained diners. In future seasons, different acts will command the showboat's stage.

Oliver's Boston terrier, Irving, says that "leaving the *Showboat Branson Belle* is a big step for a little dog, but it's good I'm going with Todd. He needs me. Look at this whole talking thing. I'll admit Todd talks for me—if he'll admit I think for him."

TAKING CANINE EXPERIENCES TO A NEW STAGE

Beginning in 2011, Todd Oliver & Friends—canines Irving, Lucy and Elvis alongside characters Pops, Miss Lilly, Joey and Oliver's Smiling Eyes Band—command the stage at noon in the Jim Stafford Theatre. In creating his act with four-footed friends, Oliver worked with two veterinarians on the safe device that fabricates the appearance of his dogs' one-line quips.

Oliver creates his characters with imagination and extra time. "Ventriloquism is a natural blessing to me," he says. "I get an idea for a character and then try to find a puppet or a dog that fits the character's face and personality. The character's voice contrasts greatly to my own. However, my little sidekicks *have* to be successful, believable characters.

"Most folks have wonderful memories of a dog," he continues, noting that his animals are family pets. "The characters I shaped for Irving and Lucy remind my audiences of people they know. One consistency in any of my shows: children, grandchildren, parents and grandparents laugh at the same jokes."

FROM SINGLE ACTS TO VARIETY

Long before Highway 76 became a famous boulevard, Branson's song soared from log cabin porches to summer picnics. Families and friends performed on flatbed trailers and in one-room schoolhouses decades before they built curtained stages enclosed by walls and a roof. Variety drove the show; no one starred. The big names stepped into the spotlight in single acts. While recognized stars still stand in the spotlight on stages in Branson—Tony Orlando, the Lennons, Mel Tillis, Daniel O'Donnell, Bobby Vinton, Andy Williams, Moe Bandy, the Oak Ridge Boys, Mickey Gilley, the Osmonds, Larry Gatlin, Ray Stevens and Jim Stafford—the variety shows have returned.

Outstanding entertainment manifests in performers who have claimed their fame in Branson. Doug Gabriel, known for his powerful voice and range, chose to pursue his performance career in the entertainment town. Once teamed with the legendary Roy Clark, Gabriel and his wife, Cheryl, perform morning shows at the Jim Stafford Theatre.

Bobby Vinton's Blue Velvet Theatre turned into Branson's Variety Theatre. Its stage hosts the Twelve Tenors and dance companies choreographed to Broadway show tunes and traditional Irish music.

Tony Orlando and the Lennons with Santa at their Christmas show. *Courtesy of Dan Lennon.*

Many single acts incorporate dancers, singers and comedians into their shows. Musician Joey Riley supports Mickey Gilley's routine, adding comic relief to Gilley's long string of hits. Clay Cooper came to Branson as a teenager with the Texas Gold Minors. While others in the group pursued different paths, Cooper stayed along 76 Country Music Boulevard, hosting *Country Tonite* before branching out to his own show, *Country Music Express*. Cooper's theater is also home to nationally known country stars Buck Trent and Neal McCoy.

The national spotlight shines on Branson today, offering entertainment for every age and preference. However, good taste for families reigns. Branson is synonymous with top talent, showmanship, creativity, patriotism and family values.

CHAPTER 13

NEW FAMILIES IN TOWN

Today in Branson there is entertainment you cannot see anywhere else. Many of these acts come in families.
—Keith Thurman, director, Shepherd of the Hills

THE HUGHES BROTHERS: THE WORLD'S LARGEST PERFORMING FAMILY

The Hughes Brothers, a family transplanted to the Ozarks from Utah, visited the Roy Clark Theatre on their first trip to Branson. Despite their grounded musical talents, they never thought that in 2002 the name Hughes American Family Theatre would replace Roy Clark's sign. The brothers honed their talents through high school and college. However, they developed varied interests that come together in Hughes Entertainment, Inc., in which they are equal partners.

During Utah summers, they developed a hard work ethic in their father's concrete fence construction business. When the family packed up and moved to Branson in 1993, they brought the fence business along. However, music soon took over.

The Hughes Brothers—Marty, Jason, Adam, Ryan and Andy—totally produce their own shows, which boast the world's largest performing family. Five brothers, five wives and twenty-seven children make up 90 percent of their forty-three-member cast. Since each brother's wife is musically accomplished, Marty jokes, "We audition our wives!"

The Hughes Brothers onstage at their Branson theater. *Courtesy of Lee Smith.*

The Hughes children onstage at their Branson theater. *Courtesy of Lee Smith.*

In addition to harmonizing, dancing and playing instruments, each brother has a hand in every aspect of the business. Family matriarch Lena Hughes wears the nametag "M&M," standing for "Mom & Manager" and indicating her role in the business end of the family's operation. The family's father runs Papa Hughes' Fudge Shop—and anything else that needs running. More than two dozen grandchildren (and counting) parade across the Hughes's stage, taking various roles as they grow. "They've been onstage since in utero," one brother says.

"We look at their participation as an opportunity for experience in a family business," Marty Hughes adds. "When one shows an interest in a particular instrument, we seek the best teacher we can find."

"We love the Ozarks," he continues. "We are reminded of the foothills of Utah with its 'benches.' But in the Utah Mountains, only wealthy people live on the 'benches.' Here, we feel as though we're living like rich folks!"

THE DUTTONS TURN A HOBBY INTO A CAREER

Dean Dutton, an economics professor who taught at universities across the country, determined that music lessons would provide the dedication and discipline to teach his children a strong work ethic. Sheila Dutton, mother of the ever-growing Dutton family, says, "We never meant to make music a full-time lifestyle."

"We all started on classical violin at a young age," Joshua, the family's youngest, posted on his blog. "At first, it was novel. Then it started to feel like hard work. But my parents, especially Mom, were as dedicated as they *wanted* me to be. Mom got up every morning to help us practice. Dad made breakfast."

Joshua remembers a bluegrass musician stopped by their house and offered to teach the family some fiddle, banjo and mandolin tunes. The Dutton Family Bluegrass Band was born.

Initially, the Duttons played as a hobby. But in 1986 they accepted an invitation to the International Children's Folk Festival in France. Suddenly, everything changed. Sheila, with no musical background, learned to play an upright bass. Dean brushed up on his guitar. When they returned from France, Dean took a temporary leave, and the family went on a nine-month American tour in which they played more than one hundred shows. The tour clarified music as their family's lifestyle. Dean gave up his teaching career to support his children in a new one.

With fifteen people and their fiddles, banjos, mandolins, a keyboard and an upright bass packed into a converted van, the family traveled more than one million miles in the United States, Canada and Europe. In addition to features on PBS and NBC, they were introduced on television in Italy, France, Germany, Spain and China. Along the way, Benjamin channeled his energy into dance; Amy picked up world champion fiddling awards and performances with symphonies; Jonathan turned into the show's comedian; Joshua added drums and harmonica to the act; Judith, Timothy and Abigail added keyboards, vocals and musicianship to the act; and they jointly became The Duttons.

In 1991, the group opened for country music artist Jerry Reed at the Lowe Family Theater. In 1997, the family chose Branson as a central—and more permanent—location. Ultimately, they purchased the BoxCar Willie Theater, which came with a motel and restaurant. All six performing Duttons married, and the family continues to grow with twenty-plus grandchildren.

In 2007, the Dutton family competed against 100,000 acts to earn a top-ten finalist slot on *America's Got Talent*. In addition to proficiently performing numerous instruments—and brightening shows with vocals and dance—each family member fills a specific role in producing the family show.

The Duttons in performance at Branson. *Courtesy of the Duttons.*

The Duttons. *Courtesy of the Duttons.*

Since 1991, the Duttons have not looked back. Although they toured the world, they embrace Branson, and the audience that now comes to see a family having fun and making music.

SIX MAKES A FULL ORCHESTRA

SIX not only harmonizes but also makes up an orchestra with their mouths. The six brothers form one of the newest family groups in Branson. From ten Knudsen sons, the six oldest (Barry, Kevin, Lynn, Jak, Owen and Curtis) surprised their father with their original songs and harmonies. Musically gifted himself, Arnold Knudsen gathered his boys around an old piano and taught them gospel hymns. Soon the youngsters were singing in four- and five-part harmony and performing in church and local civic clubs.

To this point, their background parallels the other family groups in Branson. In May 1978, they landed a debut television appearance on *The Donny and Marie Show.* However, striving to find their forte during their

SIX, with father Arnold Knudsen taking a bow. *Courtesy of Lee Smith.*

teenage years, they simultaneously competed in barbershop singing contests and punk rock concerts.

After living wherever their dad could find work to support the family, the brothers ended up in Arizona. With only a few hundred dollars between them, they determined to seek fame in California. On the streets of Los Angeles, they sang for loose change. After a few months, they scraped together enough money to rent an apartment. Gigs at parties for celebrities like Clint Eastwood and Arnold Schwarzenegger turned up. In 1988, they landed steady work at Disneyland's "Blast to the Past." During that time, they pulled together enough material to move on to better paying engagements—sharing stages with the likes of Trisha Yearwood, Diana Ross, the Beach Boys and the Doobie Brothers. They took their act on Royal Caribbean Cruise Lines and began entertaining at parties for corporate giants such as American Express, Pizza Hut, the Million Dollar Roundtable, Northeastern Financial, Pitney Bowes and Ryder Trucks.

Yet their turning point came when Las Vegas deemed them "too clean." The Knudsen brothers longed for a more stable environment for their collective nineteen children.

"In 2007, we decided to check out Branson," Barry says. "We were surprised at the friendliness—and the acceptance by its audiences."

SIX, often dubbed "an orchestra of human voices," performs at the Hughes American Family Theatre.

SIX onstage at the Hughes American Family Theatre in Branson. *Courtesy of Lee Smith.*

THE BRETT FAMILY: ON BRANSON'S CUTTING EDGE

The Brett family—dad Tom, mom Andrea and their grown children, Briahna, Brydon and Garon—carved a solid niche in Branson's music scene, starting with performances in 1999 on the *Showboat Branson Belle*. Currently, they perform their own polished two-hour production in a Branson theater, adding to the solid mix of families entertaining families. The Bretts sing, harmonize and dance to a wide variety of music from different genres and eras, blending their original songs into the act.

Music called Tom and Andrea Brett from childhood. Yet Tom trained for chiropractic services and established a successful practice. In 1996, he sustained a career-ending neck injury that sidelined him. With vision, courage and ambition, he returned to his first love—music—producing a show to include Andrea's talents as a singer/songwriter and vocal arranger.

Before playing Branson, the Bretts sang mostly a cappella, with the exception of a few ballads by Tom and Andrea, accompanied by a piano. After arriving in Branson, the couple—already musically proficient in voice and piano—expanded their act with live instrumental music and fast-paced variety. Drawing on the various strengths of each family member—Brydon

The Brett Family onstage in Branson. *Courtesy of Lee Smith.*

in rhythm and blues and big-band tunes, Briahna in country and Broadway and Garon in piano and guitar—the family pulls together a show that Brydon describes as putting one's iPod on shuffle.

Briahna Brett, the most artistically trained family member, once had her eye on Broadway or some other stardom. However, after performing in Branson, other options became less appealing. "To have the opportunity to perform with my family in a wholesome and innovative environment and to prioritize my time as a new wife and, possibly, a mother is the ideal situation for me. I get to do everything that I love in Branson."

FAMILIES ENTERTAINING FAMILIES

Some faces on Branson's stages are new; others have aged. Some families have stayed the course, while others have left their stages to follow different avenues. Yet, the backbone of entertainment in Branson remains in family shows—lifeblood that binds one generation to the next with music that intertwines hearts and settles deep in the soul.

CHAPTER 14

SIGHT & SOUND THEATER

A Business or a Ministry?

Since that "Noah Show" came to town, Branson folks no longer worry about floods. We have an ark!
—local comedian and actor Terry Sanders, when spring rains fell in torrents

Glenn Eshelman—founder, owner and executive producer of Sight & Sound Theatre—is an artist. Yet first and foremost, Eshelman describes himself as God's servant. Everything else—his paintings, his photography, his successful theaters in Pennsylvania and Missouri and his elaborate epics of biblical proportions—comes second. Often folks ask, "Are your theaters a business or a ministry?" He answers, "We are a business with a ministry."

Eshelman, based in Strasburg, Pennsylvania, says that he receives calls weekly from all over the world wanting his family to build a theater in a particular location. "We had looked at Branson," he says. "Jack and Sherry Herschend came to see *Noah: The Musical* in Strasburg. Afterward, we prayed together about our coming to Branson. But we didn't make a quick decision. However, we began to look at the Midwest—at Branson—which I term the 'Breadbasket of the Nation.'"

"My productions are for families and children," he continues, explaining that *Noah: The Musical* is a fictional presentation of the biblical account, based on Genesis chapters five through nine. "If I had seen something like *Noah* as a nine-year-old boy, it would have branded my mind for life. Today, I believe, we are branding kids' minds with things of no value. It behooves me to present to children truth and beauty. Bible stories allow people to connect...

to relate to people of faith. We portray Noah as an imperfect man, warts and all. But we show his obedience to God. Perhaps with his story, people start to think."

NOAH: THE MUSICAL STARTED WITH A JERSEY COW

Prior to 1992, Glenn Eshelman had never considered producing an epic show. "However, I had sensed that God wanted me to make a change from my multimedia presentations and staged Bible stories," he says.

> *I didn't have a clear direction until I stood in the Dairy Barn at the Harrisburg Farm Show, looking at a Jersey cow. In my heart, I heard God say, "Glenn, I want you to do a production on Noah." I questioned, "Noah?" God answered, "Yes, Noah. Look how people are drawn to animals. Look at the condition of the world."*
>
> *The words of Jesus came to me, "As it was in the days of Noah…so shall it be in the coming of the Son of Man."*

Back at home, Eshelman could not sleep. About midnight, he went to his studio. "With my Bible in one hand, and a tablet in the other, God gave me every scene in the production. I wrote and sketched furiously until daylight," he says.

Later that morning, Eshelman drove to the Strasburg Railroad Store and bought every small-scaled animal in stock. "On the fourth floor of our home, I started modeling the interior of the ark, telling no one except my wife and children. In April, I called in a leadership team."

"God wants us to produce *Noah*," I told them. "They answered, 'No way!'" However, Eshelman convinced the team that the epic could be staged. "Three of us started writing the play. Thirty-six months later, *Noah: The Musical* premiered in Strasburg. Almost two and a half million people saw the production in Pennsylvania, and now that many more are seeing it in Branson."

RISING FROM ASHES

In 1997, the Eshelmans lost their building and a majority of their equipment, sets, props and costumes in a theater fire in Pennsylvania. Within four days, Glenn Eshelman picked up a pencil and drew the building that stands

Sight & Sound Theatre, Branson, Missouri. *Courtesy of Lee Smith.*

today on a hill above Branson. In the meantime in Pennsylvania, the family built the all-new Millennium Theatre, featuring two thousand seats and a three-hundred-foot wraparound stage—a model for the Branson theater. Concurrently, the Eshelmans renovated their Living Waters Theatre to also bring live productions to that stage in Strasburg.

EXPANDING TO BRANSON

In considering an expansion to Branson, Eshelman noted that his company has a huge investment in sets from at least eleven productions presented in his Pennsylvania theaters. "Sets from *Behold the Lamb*, *The Miracle of Christmas* and *Daniel: A Dream, a Den, a Deliverer* go into storage, waiting for the show to come up again," he says. "We began thinking about wiser stewardship and using our resources in another location. Also, starting an additional venue gives opportunity for people to earn their bread and butter at something that changes the lives and the destiny of people."

Construction of the building in Branson took three and a half years to complete. "We used tons and tons of steel and concrete, miles and miles of wire and conduit, sheet after sheet of drywall and foam insulation, over five hundred doors, rubber roofing, ceiling ductwork and plumbing, phone systems, wall plaster, décor, paint, trees in the lobby [and] fiberglass domes," Eshelman continues. "All of this translated to jobs in the Ozarks."

The Eshelman family includes wife Shirley, four daughters, fourteen grandchildren and two great-grandchildren. The daughters and two sons-in-law work in some capacity at the company. "My children are as tight and tough as Pop," Eshelman says. "They get right in the dirt with me. When I'm at Branson, I help mow the grass, clip the weeds and plant the flowers. I never ask an employee to do anything I don't do myself."

HUMBLE BEGINNINGS

Glenn and Shirley Eshelman started their life together as dairy farmers. They still live on a Pennsylvania farm. "I'm a man of the dirt; I was born into it, live in it and someday, I plan to return to it," Eshelman says. "My tractor is my ivory palace, and my farm is my golf course. Animals and farming are very much a part of my life."

"As a farmer, my dad taught me to save seed from each crop to plant the next year," he continues. "Now, instead of tending cows in a barn, we put on productions that entertain and minister to families. We've always taken the seed from any production and reinvested it in another production or theater. We plow everything back into the ministry."

Eshelman believes that God created his ministry show by show, dollar by dollar and building by building. The Eshelmans started Sight & Sound Theatre in Pennsylvania during the summer of 1975 in a rented auditorium, presenting a ten-week multimedia show of Glenn's artwork titled *The Wonder of It All*. Based on that success, they built the original Sight & Sound Theatre, which is now Living Waters Theatre in Strasburg.

"The first theater required a $100,000 loan, which was huge for us," Eshelman states. "Over the years, Shirley and I have done what we could do, using what we had at the time."

In July 1976, the Sight & Sound Theatre opened for the performance of *A Land of Our Own*. Live actors and actresses were eventually added to the productions, and *Behold the Lamb* debuted in 1987 as the first full-length live stage production at the original theater. A larger facility, the Sight & Sound Entertainment Centre, opened in March 1991.

THE CHRISTIAN BROADWAY

Sight & Sound Theatre has been described as "the largest faith-based live theater in America" and "one of the top three theater destinations on the East Coast," as well as the "Christian Broadway." Each year, about 800,000 people come from around the country and the world to experience live Bible-based performances in the Pennsylvania theaters. An equal number now visit the Sight & Sound Theatre in Branson.

Building a show takes two to three years. A storyline is developed, scripts are written, sets and costumes are designed and built and music and choreography are created. Eshelman explains that vocal performances, both singing and speaking, are live for all shows. However, for most of the productions, the instrumental music is written specifically for a show and then recorded in a professional studio. On occasion, instrumentalists appear onstage, and their performances are live.

Most shows run for a predetermined length of time before being replaced by a different production. *Noah: The Musical* opened the Branson theater in 2008. The *Miracle of Christmas* took over the Christmas season in 2009, but *Noah* returned in the spring of 2010.

NOAH'S ARK IN BRANSON

As *Noah: The Musical* unfolds on a three-hundred-foot wraparound stage in Branson's Sight & Sound Theatre, the audience watches a forty-foot-tall ark take shape. The massive fly space permits rotating set pieces enhanced with three-dimensional video imaging, pyrotechnics and laser lighting in special effects. After intermission, curtains raise to reveal the interior of the huge ark, four stories tall and filled with live and animatronic creatures. Many of the animals, trained and housed in special quarters at the theater, trek down the aisles and up the ramp of the ark—two by two, of course. Theatergoers experience the tension of Noah's family closing the ark's door when rain begins to fall. They sense the lurching and rolling of the huge vessel as waters cover the earth. The daily monotonous task of feeding earth's numerous species plays out on three sides of the audience, drawing observers into the heightening stress of Noah's family, confined for months in a huge wooden boat.

When their trying journey ends, the play's finale explodes onstage with changing scenery—and the revelation of God's reward for Noah's unquestioning obedience and devotion to him.

Noah: The Musical at Sight & Sound Theatre, Branson, Missouri. *Courtesy of Sight & Sound Theatre.*

"I believe in producing beauty and excellence, but so people will say, 'I've never seen anything like that before,'" Eshelman says. "People said that about Jesus Christ. They had never seen anything like him before."

He acknowledges that in Branson his family is drinking from wells they never dug and building on foundations that others formed. "However, we hope we can dig new wells, plant new trees and build on the foundations already formed," he says.

"We didn't come into the area any different from anyone else starting a business," Eshelman continues. "I don't mimic others. I am totally dependent on receiving my direction from God. It takes work and discipline, and we don't have an edge on God. Yet, he has promised that we have not because we ask not."

Like countless families before them, Glenn and Shirley Eshelman came to the Ozarks to put down roots, entertain families and contribute to the community of Branson. They hope that the larger-than-life productions they present go beyond entertainment to give God's message of redemption and hope to their audiences.

Resources

The Beverly Hillbillies. DVD. Silver Dollar City Edition. Branson, Missouri. CBS Broadcast System, Special Edition, 2010 (originally filmed in 1969).

Branson Area—Marvel Cave postcards. www.hbw.addr.com/marvelcavepc. htm.

Edwards, Mike W. "Through Ozark Hills and Hollows." *National Geographic* (November 1970): 656.

Foggy River Boys. www.mikepatrick.com/FRB.htm.

"The History and Science of Marvel Cave." www.bransonsilverdollarcity. com/group-travel/MarvelCave.pdf.

LaRoe, Lisa Moore. "Ozarks Harmony." *National Geographic* (April 1998): 76.

Lynn, Bud. *The History: Those Who Walked With Wright.* 1st ed. Galena, MO: Ozark Trails Magazine, Inc., 1985. Tenth edition, September 1999.

Mabe, Brent. *The Baldknobbers: The Making of an Ozarks Legend.* Cassville, MO: Litho Printers & Bindery, 2009.

Madsen, Jerry S. *Branson: A Time for History.* Galena, MO: Ozark Trails Magazine, Inc., 1997.

Mahnkey, Douglas. "Alf Bolin's Buried Treasure." *White River Valley Historical Quarterly* 5, no. 6 (Winter 1974). http://thelibrary.springfield.missouri.org/lochist/periodicals/wrv/V5/N6/w74a.html.

Marr, Ron. *The Presley Family Story. Missouri Life, Inc.* Boonville, MO: Presleys' Inc., 2008.

Martin, Ronald L. *Jewel of the Ozarks: Marvel Cave.* Springfield, MO: Ozark Mountain Publishers, 1974, 1990.

Marvel Cave. DVD. Branson, Missouri. FAN Productions, 2005.

Marvel Cave. Springfield, MO: Ozark Mountain Publishers, 1974, 1990.

"Marvel Cave." Wikipedia. www.en.wikipedia.org/wiki/Marvel_Cave.

Missouri Department of Conservation Online. www.mdc.mo.gov/conmag/1998/12/20.htm. Author of the article "S. Fred Prince," Suzanne Wilson, a freelance writer and editor, lives near Joplin. She has written for the *Conservationist* about such subjects as bird eggs, cave divers, wildlife photography and armadillos.

MPHS—St. Louis Iron Mountain & Southern Railway. www.mopac.org/history_stlims.asp.
The Osmonds: America's Favorite Family of Entertainment. http://osmond.com.

"The Osmonds." Wikipedia. http://en.wikipedia.org/wiki/The_Osmonds.

Owen, Luella Agnes. *Cave Regions of the Ozarks and Black Hills.* Cincinnati, OH: Editor Publishing Company, 1898. Reprinted: General Books, 2010.

"Ozark Jubilee." http://en.wikipedia.org/wiki/Ozark_Jubilee.

Payton, Leland, and Crystal Payton. *The Story of Silver Dollar City.* 1st ed. Springfield, MO: Lens & Pens Production, 1997. Revised, 1999. 2nd ed., 2007.

Prince, S. Fred, assisted by William T. Lynch. "The Story of Marvel Caverns." Also called "The Cave Book." Parts of the unpublished manuscript were written and sketched in 1894 and years following. Parts were written in 1935–37. Branson, Missouri. The work cannot be found except in the archives of Silver Dollar City. His granddaughter, Charlotte Al-hujazi, Washington, D.C., owns the rights to the manuscript.

The Shepherd of the Hills. www.oldmatt.com.

Show Caves of the United States of America: Marvel Cave. www.showcaves. com/english/usa/showcaves/Marvel.html.

Spurlock, Pearl. *Over the Old Ozark Trails in the Shepherd of the Hills Country.* Branson, MO: White River Leader, 1936.

Stone County News-Oracle articles. www.eons.com/groups/topic/831397-Stone-County-New-Oracle.

Sylvester, Ron, with Jeff Hampton. *Branson: Onstage in the Ozarks.* Fort Worth, TX: Summit Group, 1994.

Tony Orlando's Official Web Site. www.tonyorlando.com.

MARVEL CAVE

The following document comes transcribed from the *Stone County News-Oracle* 33, no. 41 (January 2, 1918): 4, col. 5.

Information on the site:
Marvel Cave for Lease.
To the end of devoting a part, at least, of the time to National service, in special ways that will help, I am open to negotiations for leasing Marvel Cave. The time is opportune. I have just completed a new road of easy grade to Roark Station, which gives excellent auto service, for railroad connection, and on to Springfield. An inviting business opportunity for the right parties. Address,
WM. H. LYNCH
Reeds Spring, MO

INDEX

ABOUT THE AUTHOR

Arline Chandler left a teaching career in the kindergarten classroom to launch full time into writing. She combines RV travel with her interest in people and places and their history. Her numerous articles have been published in *Workamper News*, *Branson's Review*, *Motorhome*, *Ozarks Mountaineer*, *Ozarks Magazine*, *Mature Living*, *Coast to Coast* magazine and other entertainment, travel and senior adult publications.

Chandler served as an instructor at the University of Idaho's annual "Life on Wheels" RV conference from 1995 to 2005 and was a featured speaker for the Rally, an annual RVing event held at various locations around the United States. Her most recent book, *Truly Zula: Daughter of the Ozarks*, recounts the life and experiences of her aunt, the late Zula Turney. Chandler's essay "A Teacher for Life" is one of fifty in an anthology entitled *My Teacher Is My Hero*, published by Adams Media in 2008.

When not on the road, she and her photographer husband, Lee Smith, make their home in the Ozarks foothills at Heber Springs, Arkansas. Information about her life and books is available at www.arlinechandler.com and www.arlinechandler.blogspot.com.

Visit us at
www.historypress.net